Buddha Nature

Buddha Nature

Ten Teachings on
The Uttara Tantra Shastra

Thrangu Rinpoche

FOREWORD BY CHÖKYI NYIMA RINPOCHE

TRANSLATED BY ERIK PEMA KUNSANG

EDITED BY S. LHAMO

RANGJUNG YESHE PUBLICATIONS

Rangjung Yeshe Publications
Flat 2C Hattan Place
1 A Po Shan Road, Hong Kong

Address letters to:

Rangjung Yeshe Publications
Ka-Nying Shedrub Ling Monastery
P.O. Box 1200, Kathmandu, Nepal

9 8 7 6 5 4 3 2 1

Second revised edition 1993

Printed in the United States of America on recycled acid-free
paper

Publication Data:

Thrangu Rinpoche, Khenchen (b. 1933). Foreword by Chökyi
Nyima Rinpoche (b. 1951). Translated from the Tibetan by Erik
Pema Kunsang (Erik Hein Schmidt). Edited by S. Lhamo. 2nd ed.
Title: Buddha Nature (The Seed of Happiness)
isbn 962-7341-17-7 (pbk.)
1. Uttara Tantra Shastra, commentary on. 2. Mahayana
philosophy — Buddhism. 3. Buddhism — Tibet. I. Title.

Cover design by Brigid Ryan
Cover photo by Noah Gordon

Contents

Foreword

In the spring of 1985, I approached Venerable Khenchen Thrangu Rinpoche with a request. At that time, many Western students of Tibetan Buddhism were studying at the monasteries which surround the village of Boudhanath. Because this excellent teacher, Thrangu Rinpoche, was present at his monastery adjacent to the Great Stupa, a very hallowed place of pilgrimage in Nepal, it seemed the ideal time to gather the students together. I asked Rinpoche to teach Lord Maitreya's important treatise, the *Uttara Tantra Shastra*. To my delight, Rinpoche agreed to comment on this very profound and lucid text.

Each morning for twelve days, Rinpoche opened his personal shrine room to more than sixty enthusiastic students, including myself, who listened quietly while he carefully explained each chapter of the text. At the end of every teaching, Rinpoche held a frank and lighthearted question and answer session. His presentation was invaluable.

Venerable Khenchen Thrangu Rinpoche was born in Tibet in 1933. When a small boy, His Holiness, the Gyalwa Karmapa, recognized him as the ninth incarnation of a great bodhisattva. Thrangu Rinpoche began his formal training at a very young age and, at twenty-three, received his Gelong ordination, together with Chögyam Trungpa Rinpoche, from His Holiness Karmapa. Shortly after, he moved to Rumtek, the Seat of the Kagyü lineage. In 1968, he took his Geshe examination which was witnessed by 1500 monks from all parts of India. He was awarded the degree of *Geshe Rabjam* and was appointed vice-chancellor of the Principle Seat of the Kagyü, as

Vajra-holder of the Three Precepts. He also holds a direct lineage of the special *Shentong* philosophical tradition. Furthermore, he was named Khenpo of Rumtek and all the Kagyü sect and became the Abbot of Rumtek Monastery. Rinpoche then took on the role of personal teacher of the four main lineage-holders — Shamar Rinpoche, Situ Rinpoche, Jamgön Kongtrül Rinpoche, and Gyaltsab Rinpoche — as well as the scores of young monks and tulkus residing at Rumtek.

Since that time, Rinpoche has traveled extensively throughout Southeast Asia, Europe, and the United States to give teachings on Tibetan Buddhism. His playful, yet straightforward and brilliant, oral teachings have endeared him to his Western audiences. At present, he is abbot of his own monastery in Boudhanath, Thrangu Tashi Chöling, and founder of a retreat center at Namo Buddha, in the foothills of Kathmandu Valley. In addition, he holds the title of abbot at Gampo Abbey, the late Venerable Trungpa Rinpoche's newly established monastery, in Cape Breton, Nova Scotia.

I believe I speak for all who were present at this impromptu seminar when expressing my deep appreciation for the thoughtful exposition given by this highly realized master. May this teaching not pass away, but benefit all beings everywhere.

Chökyi Nyima Rinpoche
Boudhanath, Nepal
Summer, 1988

Introduction

In general, a person is considered sensible and even honorable when he strives to benefit himself, but sometimes people intend to harm others in order to gain happiness for themselves. In the context of Dharma, this is called a 'wrong intention.' A 'good intention' is simply the wish to benefit others. Nevertheless, if we interpret the word 'others' to indicate only a select few, like our friends, relatives, and countrymen, then our intention is biased. We should never be partial to some beings while harming others; instead, we should try to cultivate an attitude that embraces all sentient beings with good wishes, including animals. In this way, our good intentions will develop into all-encompassing *bodhichitta*.

Some say that the Buddhists are not really serving society. For example, Christian organizations build schools and hospitals. From this point of view, it may indeed appear as though the Buddhists are not working in a concrete way to benefit the community. Yet, the main objective of Buddhism is to accomplish the welfare of others through practices engaged in mentally. The Buddhist practitioner serves others through his good intentions. Perpetuating wholesome motives, he or she can truly benefit beings. Therefore, whether we are listening to Dharma teachings, reading about them, or putting them into practice, it is extremely important to develop the attitude of bodhichitta.

Although we plan to search out and follow the true and perfect path, without a qualified guide we will never discover this path. If we try to find the path by ourselves or follow an imperfect teacher, we are in danger of making a grave mistake. Therefore, we must first carefully seek out a genuine spiritual master and then adhere to his advice.

To prove that this teaching was originally taught by a fully qualified master, the title is given first in Sanskrit. This indicates that the teachings were originally presented in India by the Enlightened One himself, Buddha Shakyamuni.

The full Sanskrit title of our text is *Mahayana Uttara Tantra Shastra* while the Tibetan title is *Tegpa Chenpo Gyü Lamey Tenchö*. The word *shastra* means 'treatise,' but Tibetan scholars translated this as *tenchö* which means 'showing and changing' — to show the path to changing the disturbing emotions and unwholesome habits that exist in one's being. Therefore, *shastra* actually means 'showing the true path and changing one's disturbing emotions.' Altogether, the shastra indicates that our disturbing emotions are transformed by entering the correct path.

In Tibetan, this treatise is popularly known as the *Gyü Lama*. Both the Sanskrit *uttara* and the Tibetan word *lama* mean highest or unexcelled. The teaching is described this way because it belongs to the Third Turning of the Wheel of Dharma. The second part of the title is *tantra, gyü* in Tibetan. Often the word tantra calls to mind something to do with channels, energies, or sexual practices, but this is not the real meaning of the word tantra. Tantra means 'that which continues,' the continuation of what exists at the time of the *ground,* at the time of traversing the *path,* and at the time of attaining the *fruition.* Therefore, the word tantra should be understood to mean 'continuity.' In short, Uttara Tantra means 'Unexcelled Continuity.'

The main theme of our text, the *Uttara Tantra Shastra,* examines something each of us possess — *buddha nature.* We each have the seed of enlightenment within ourselves and because this potential can be actualized, it is said that we possess an enlightened essence.

The text opens with an inquiry into the principal topics which constitute the body of the teaching. The main topic is called the *real condition.* In order to explain this real condition, the basic state of affairs, it is first taught that *samsara,* conditioned existence, is replete with various kinds of suffering. Why do these miseries arise? What is their source? Suffering originates with mistakenness, delusion. The five predominant disturbing emotions: anger, attachment, stupidity, pride, and jealousy are based on ignorance, a lack of knowing, which arises due to our misunderstanding of the real condition — the way things truly are. To clear away this confusion and ignorance, we must realize the true nature of things.

The Buddha gave graduated teachings to help sentient beings recognize this real condition — the nature of things. In general, people believe that the world is permanent and capable of offering lasting happiness. To abolish this mistaken concept, at the outset Lord Buddha slightly concealed the real condition of things. His initial teachings, which characterized this world as having the nature of impermanence and suffering, are called the *First Turning of the Wheel of Dharma.*

After his students had familiarized themselves with these fundamental teachings, the Buddha taught that although the truth of impermanence is undeniable, it also has no concrete existence. Thus, he explained the *Second Turning of the Wheel of Dharma* which emphasizes emptiness — that all things lack both concrete substance and self-nature.

Later on, the Buddha taught that emptiness does not signify a mere state of blankness. If that were the case, how could any phenomena appear at all? How could an entire universe arise? At that point, he taught the last set of teachings — the *Third Turning of the Wheel of Dharma* which accentuates the luminous aspect of mind, the ability to know all manifested things. This profound, ultimate teaching emphasizes wisdom, innate wakefulness.

Vajrayana is said to be swifter and more powerful than Mahayana, but prior to giving Vajrayana teachings the Buddha taught the Mahayana vehicle. In order to practice Vajrayana teachings, one must first establish the basis for practice which is twofold: arousing bodhichitta and resolving the correct view. Without a firm foundation in these two aspects, one cannot truly practice the path of Vajrayana.

Lord Buddha gave a vast number of Sutra and Tantra teachings. This treatise belongs to the category of Sutra. Although the Buddha gave a wide variety of Sutra teachings, he started by giving advice which emphasized the benefits for oneself. These are the focal point of Hinayana, the lesser vehicle. Later, the Buddha presented teachings which stress the attempt to attain enlightenment for the benefit of all sentient beings equal in number to the vastness of the sky. These are featured in the Mahayana vehicle. The Uttara Tantra is a Mahayana teaching.

Although this teaching belongs to Mahayana, the word 'tantra' is included in the title. The reason for this is that at the time of the ground, when one is still a sentient being, one possesses *buddha nature,* the potential for enlightenment. At the time of the path, when one becomes a bodhisattva, the enlightened essence continues. At the time of fruition — complete buddhahood — the sugata-essence continues still. Since the enlightened essence is a continuity that extends throughout our journey along the stages of ground, path, and fruition, it is called *tantra* — continuity.

Beings on the path to enlightenment are grouped as belonging to one of three stages: impure, partly pure and partly impure, and utterly pure. How is the enlightened essence when one is an ordinary impure being? What is it like when one is partly pure and partly impure, a bodhisattva? Finally, what is the enlightened essence like when one attains absolute purity, complete enlightenment? These three categories, which explain the enlightened essence's characteristics at different stages of the path to enlightenment, are the main topics of discourse in the Uttara Tantra.

To which category of teaching does the Uttara Tantra taught by Lord Maitreya belong? It belongs to the Third Turning of the Wheel of Dharma. The information contained in this text is based on the *Dharani Raja Sutra,* a teaching given by the Buddha. Although this teaching had already been presented in the *Dharani Raja Sutra,* Lord Maitreya summarized it in this clear and lucid treatise.

The Uttara Tantra is considered a Buddhist teaching, but we cannot say it is the word of the Buddha, himself. Buddhist teachings are usually grouped under two headings:

— teachings actually given by the Buddha himself, and
— teachings given with the Buddha's permission.

In the second instance, the Buddha has told a person, "You are allowed to give such and such teaching to other beings." Since the Buddha, himself, authorized Lord Maitreya as his Dharma regent, there is no contradiction in saying that this is a teaching given indirectly by the Buddha.

The calibre of an author of Buddhist scripture is usually categorized as either superior, intermediate, or lesser. Ideally, a composition is authored by one who has directly perceived the truth of reality, of *dharmata.* Having realized the nature of things, he or she is, therefore, capable of giving lucid teachings about reality. The intermediate composer has received permission and guidance from his or her personal *yidam*, the meditation deity. For example, if one experienced a vision of the Bodhisattva Manjushri and received the command to compose a particular teaching, then even if one were unable to perceive the truth of reality, under the yidam's guidance and inspiration one would still be able to render a valid composition. One's faults would be dispelled while writing. In the last case, a qualified composer is one erudite in the Buddha's teachings as well as the *five sciences*. One is then capable of composing a treatise.

Lord Maitreya

Lord Maitreya, regent of the fully enlightened Buddha Shakyamuni, composed the Uttara Tantra. Therefore, the author of our text belongs to the highest classification, the best of the best. Not only has Lord Maitreya perceived the truth of reality, but he attained the tenth bodhisattva *bhumi* and was empowered by Buddha Shakyamuni to be his successor.

Unexcelled in composition, Lord Maitreya transmitted this teaching to his disciple, Arya Asanga. The *Manjushri Mula Tantra* prophesied that one named Arya Asanga would someday appear. Moreover, Buddha Shakyamuni predicted that the monk, Asanga, would clarify and establish both the expedient and the definitive meaning of the scriptures.

Arya Asanga

As predicted, Asanga appeared and undertook the practice of meditating upon Maitreya for twelve years. Initially, Asanga practiced for three years, but nothing happened and he thought, "I have undergone so much hardship. I've practiced diligently, but it has been fruitless." In despair, he left his retreat and wandered off. Along the road, he met a man polishing an iron bar with his bare hands. Asanga asked, "What are you doing?" and the man replied, "I'm trying to make a sewing needle." Asanga thought to himself, "He's making a needle from an iron bar. What diligence! Compared to him, my diligence is nothing. I must go back and practice."

Nine years elapsed and Asanga again felt that his practice was of no avail. Thinking he had accomplished nothing, he left his place of retreat. Wandering the countryside, he noticed a dog laying in the road. The animal had numerous sores which were infested with maggots in the lower part of its body. Seeing this, Asanga felt immense compassion. He thought, "If I try to remove the maggots with my fingers, they will die, but if I don't take them out the dog will die." So he took out his knife and cut a piece of flesh from his own thigh. He placed it beside the dog. To avoid harming the worms, Asanga was about to lick them out of the wounds with his tongue and put them on the other piece of flesh. He could not bear to look, so he closed his eyes and put out his tongue as he bent down to lick off the maggots, but his tongue touched bare earth instead of the dog. Asanga opened his eyes. The dog had vanished and, instead, Maitreya appeared before him. Asanga cried out, "Maitreya! You have no compassion. I have practiced so hard for twelve years and you never appeared. Why didn't you come?" Maitreya replied, "I've always been right beside you, but your obscurations prevented you from seeing me. Now, because of your great compassion, the last obscuration has been purified and you can see that I'm here."

After their meeting, Asanga accompanied Maitreya to his dwelling place in Tushita Heaven where he received the renowned Five Teachings Of Maitreya. The first teaching, called *Ornament of Realization (Abhisamaya Lamkara)*, clarifies the Second Turning of the Wheel of Dharma. The next three teachings are general works given to clarify all of Buddha Shakyamuni's teachings. These are called *Ornament of the Sutras (Sutra Lamkara)*, *Discerning the Middle and the Extremes*, and *Discerning Dharmas and Dharmata*. The fifth work taught by Lord Maitreya truly establishes the Third Turning of the Wheel of Dharma. It is the *Uttara Tantra*.

Asanga passed the first three sections of the Five Teachings of Maitreya on to his own disciples, but he considered the latter two sections of teachings — *Discerning Dharmas and Dharmata* and the *Uttara Tantra* — too profound for people of that day and age to readily understand. Therefore, he concealed them as treasures. Later on, they were rediscovered and revealed by Maitripa, guru of Marpa the Translator. After the master, Maitripa, revealed these teachings which had been hidden as treasures, he had a vision of Maitreya who appeared before him amidst a gathering of clouds. At that time, Maitripa received the complete transmission and instructions on these texts. Afterwards, Maitripa propagated this teaching widely.

Homage

In the beginning of a translated scripture, the translator pays homage to the lineage gurus. The Uttara Tantra opens with: "Homage to all the buddhas and bodhisattvas." The translator placed the homage at the very beginning of the text to facilitate his completion of the translation without any obstacles or interruptions.

The title and the translator's homage were not part of the teaching given by Maitreya, himself, nor part of the original Sanskrit text. They were inserted later on by the translator, Loden Sherab. In Tibet, a translator often inserted his own personal homage in a text invoking the blessings of whichever deity he felt especially inclined towards. Eventually, the king of Tibet ruled that all teachings which could be classified as belonging to the section of Buddhist literature known as *Abhidharma* must begin with: "Homage to noble Manjushri" and that teachings falling into the category of *Vinaya* must commence with "Homage to the Omniscient One."

The Uttara Tantra belongs mainly to the Sutra classification, the Third Turning of the Wheel of Dharma, because the text contains sections concerning the view, path, and fruition as well as many other topics. In combination, they are classified as Sutra because the word 'Sutra' literally means 'confluence' or 'that which has many parts gathered together.' Since it emphasizes the enlightened essence, the sugata-essence, and because it is inseparable from the very basis of *Mahamudra*, this teaching is considered of great importance in the *Kagyü* tradition.

The teaching has two lines of transmission: the system of expounding and the system of meditating on the teachings of Maitreya. Both have reached us through Jamgön Kongtrül the First. Presented here is a system which is mainly utilized to teach the Uttara Tantra to practitioners of Mahamudra.

The Rangtong and Shentong Systems

In general, this treatise may be explained through either the *Rangtong* system, which emphasizes the empty aspect of the enlightened essence, or the *Shentong* system, which stresses the wisdom aspect of the enlightened essence. Today, we will follow the method of Shentong, emphasizing the wisdom aspect.

The Rangtong system follows the avenue of reasoning by which the real condition is easily resolved through logic. Because it is more convenient, many masters follow the Rangtong method. But when actually putting the teachings into practice, overstressing the empty aspect sometimes creates problems. Contemplating emptiness in the analytical style of a pandita, one merely thinks, "This is emptiness," or "Emptiness is such and such," which is a mere mental construct. One has not actually perceived emptiness and therefore Rangtong is a stage on the gradual path.

In the Shentong system, the practitioner is urged to rest in the natural state, the luminous nature of mind. Therefore, the wisdom or wakefulness aspect is emphasized.

In terms of scholarship, the pandita method, or the Rangtong system, is said to be rapid, but in terms of actual practice the Shentong system is faster. This second method is called the technique of a simple meditator, a *kusulu*. Since the Kagyü tradition stresses the meditation technique of a simple meditator, the view of Shentong is regarded as more profound.

The Seven Vajra Topics

Seven vajra topics are contained in the body of our text. 'Vajra' means solid and firm. The vajra can defeat all opponents without harming the wielder. In other words, when one realizes these teachings, all ignorance and misunderstanding is destroyed.

The first three vajra topics, the Three Jewels, refer to the fruition:

1 — The Buddha.
2 — The Dharma.
3 — The Sangha.

The next four vajra topics are called the *four inconceivable vajra points:*

4 — Buddha nature.
5 — Enlightenment.
6 — Qualities.
7 — Activities.

The cause for this fruition is our buddha nature itself, the sugata-essence. Possessing this cause, or seed, one can attain the fifth topic, enlightenment. When attaining enlightenment, certain qualities manifest. These enlightened qualities are the sixth topic. Endowed with the enlightened qualities, buddha activity naturally follows. These enlightened activities are the seventh topic. In brief, the Seven Vajra Topics constitute the body of this treatise.

1 — The Buddha

The first vajra topic is the Buddha, himself, whom we identify as our main teacher because he possesses two very special qualities. In the original Sanskrit, *buddha* means 'enlightened' or, literally, 'perfected in knowledge.' In Tibetan, the word 'buddha' is *sangye*. *Sang* means 'purified' or 'cleared away,' meaning that all defects and faults, such as the disturbing emotions and karmas, have been completely purified and removed. *Gye* means 'unfolded' or 'fully developed,' meaning that the Enlightened One has fully developed all the wisdoms and virtues of the enlightened qualities.

2 — The Dharma

The second vajra topic, Dharma, in Tibetan *chö*, has many different connotations, but it mainly means 'to change or remedy something.' What is remedied? The unwholesome habits and inclinations that we have perpetuated since beginningless time. Through Dharma practice our unwholesome intentions, which we have been accustomed to for so long, are changed into positive, beneficial actions.

3 — The Sangha

When translated into Tibetan, the third vajra topic, sangha, became *tsok*, or *gendün*, and took on the literal meaning 'group' or 'assembly,' but a deeper meaning is implied. *Gendün* means 'intent on the virtuous,' and 'to strive for what is good,' but actually the idea comes closer to a kind of potential. We have the ability or potential for attaining enlightenment. Without this potential, liberation would be impossible. For example, can gold be extracted from sand? No, because sand does not have the potential to yield gold, but gold ore can be melted and gold obtained. Likewise, when churned, milk has the potential to yield butter. In accordance with these two analogies, because of possessing the enlightened essence, sentient beings have the natural potential to attain enlightenment. Therefore, not only is it possible to attain enlightenment, but it is necessary that we do so.

4 — Buddha Nature

There is a direct link between the fourth and fifth vajra topics, buddha nature and enlightenment. Right now, the enlightened essence is obscured by the defects of disturbing emotions, but these can be purified. Once defilements have been cleared away, one automatically attains liberation from samsara.

5 — Enlightenment

The Sanskrit word *bodhi* means 'enlightenment.' In Tibetan, this is *jang-chub*. The meaning is almost the same as *buddha,* except there is a slightly different feeling to it. *Jang* means 'purified' — all the disturbing emotions and karmas have been purified and all that must be abandoned has been abandoned. *Chub* means 'perfected' or 'developed,' referring to the enlightened qualities, knowledge, and so forth. Yet, both *buddha* and *bodhi* refer to the fruition of the path.

6 — Qualities

The sixth vajra topic describes the qualities of enlightenment. After practicing on the path, abandoning what should be abandoned, and developing what should be developed, what is attained? Some kind of qualities should manifest. If butter had no purpose, churning milk with tremendous exertion would be pointless. Likewise, if we study, practice, and withstand a great deal of hardship to attain enlightenment, a worthwhile fruition should result which validates our efforts.

7 — Buddha Activity

Will buddha qualities benefit sentient beings? Attaining enlightenment for oneself alone would not seem quite right. A king possesses great power and vast dominion, but if he doesn't benefit his subjects, they will revolt. Likewise, after attaining enlightenment, enlightened activities which manifest for the welfare of others are effortlessly and spontaneously present. This is the seventh vajra topic — buddha activity.

Studying the first three vajra topics, one will discover the virtues of the Three Jewels. Studying the four latter topics, one will discover the path to accomplish them, oneself.

Buddha

There are two types of refuge: the refuge of causation and the refuge of fruition. Usually, the refuge of causation refers to instances of taking refuge in the Three Jewels, such as when practicing the preliminaries. One takes refuge in Buddha Shakyamuni, identifying him as the supreme teacher, and trusting that no one else can guide one on the path to liberation. Taking refuge in a perfect guide, one becomes a qualified student. If one becomes his disciple, one must firmly resolve to follow the teacher and his path. Thus, one becomes eligible to progress along the path and thereby attain the fruition, buddhahood. This method of taking refuge is called the refuge of causation.

In the Uttara Tantra, refuge is explained in terms of fruition. The phrase refuge of fruition implies the final result — the future state of enlightenment — which liberates one from the ocean of samsara and accomplishes perfect happiness and ease. Right now, we should learn how to practice and attain this refuge of fruition.

Ordinarily, we say, "I take refuge in the Buddha." But there is a slight difference between this Buddha and the Buddha described in the Uttara Tantra. Perhaps, we should say that the Buddha in the Uttara Tantra is actually a description of the state of buddhahood, itself.

Why should we strive to attain buddhahood? The state of enlightenment is endowed with two specific benefits: the perfect benefit for oneself and the perfect benefit for others. According to our text, there are six subsidiary qualities, as well.

The state of complete buddhahood is:

1 — Uncreated;
2 — Spontaneously present;
3 — Not realized through external causes;
4 — Possessed of knowledge;
5 — Compassionate love;
6 — Abilities.

Among these six, the first three are called the three perfect qualities which benefit oneself:

1 — Uncreated

The quality of being uncreated, or unformed means that buddhahood is not a compound, a constructed state. Usually, a compound is made up of an assemblage of different parts like the construction of an airplane. No matter how permanent and solid such an object may seem, someday we'll say, "The airplane doesn't work anymore," or "It fell down," or "It was destroyed." An airplane is constructed by assembling the frame, the machinery, the electrical wiring, and so forth. It may have a very high value, but sooner or later it will disintegrate. Likewise, all compounded phenomena, whatever is created by parts coming together, are impermanent. No matter how much effort one exerts trying to maintain a lasting existence, it will always be fruitless. Therefore, one strives to attain the uncompounded, unproduced state of complete enlightenment.

Buddhahood expresses itself as the three kayas: *dharmakaya, sambhogakaya,* and *nirmanakaya.* The uncompounded aspect of buddhahood refers to the dharmakaya. Why is the dharmakaya of buddhahood uncreated, not a product? From one standpoint, the dharmakaya seems to be a state that must be achieved through attaining enlightenment, as though we are *not* now enlightened and do not, at present, possess the dharmakaya. But from another viewpoint, the term dharmakaya refers to the realization of what we already naturally possess — the enlightened essence, the potential for buddhahood. From that angle, the dharmakaya of buddhahood is not produced. It is natural and uncreated. Since the enlightened essence is uncreated, the experience of buddhahood is, therefore, changeless and permanent.

2 — Spontaneously Present

The second quality of buddhahood is that it is spontaneously present. When we hear that buddhahood is uncreated, we might think it is devoid of any qualities whatsoever. The essence of space is completely blank, uncompounded, and devoid of any desirable qualities, but enlightenment is endowed with immeasurable qualities which are spontaneously present.

3 — Not Realized Through External Causes

The third quality of buddhahood is that it is not realized through external causes. How does one realize a state of being which is both uncreated and spontaneously present? These two qualities are not realized by any extraneous cause. If they were, one would have to rely on an outside agent to attain realization. In that case, one could only achieve enlightenment while under the influence of another person or thing. But buddhahood is attained by merely realizing what one already possesses, the enlightened essence within oneself. Therefore, realization does not rely or depend upon any substantial cause external to oneself.

This explains the three perfect qualities which benefit oneself, but if buddhahood were attained just to benefit oneself it would not be so extraordinary. Still, the three qualities which benefit others are dependent upon the 'three qualities which benefit oneself.' Therefore, in our text they appear subsequently.

The next three are called the three perfect qualities which benefit others.

4 — Possessed of Knowledge

The compassion of buddhahood is endowed with the knowledge that sees clearly what sentient beings need and knows how to benefit them. For example, some years ago America felt very kindly towards the country of Vietnam and wanted to help the inhabitants. Americans gave a tremendous amount of aid in various ways, but they were ultimately unable to save the Vietnamese and it might even seem that the aid was actually harmful. This was because the people's kindness was not founded in perfect knowledge. I apologize to the Americans present. [Laughter]

The quality of perfect knowledge perceives the suffering of beings exactly as it is and knows how to actually relieve or protect beings from these miseries. Based on this perception or knowledge, compassionate love arises and from that the capacity to benefit beings springs forth.

5 — Compassionate Love

"Where does this capacity come from?" It originates with the great compassionate love which the Buddha possesses for all living beings. Compassionate love is a natural remedy. Its antithesis, hatred and ill-will, are natural poisons. For example, if a person becomes easily angered or is hateful or spiteful, others will shun him, thinking, "I should stay away from that person." On the other hand, when someone is kind and loving, others will think, "This is my friend. I like him. I want to help him." One hundred evil-minded or short-tempered people will appear to oneself as one hundred enemies whereas the same number of kind and compassionate people will be regarded as friends. The reason why the Buddha was able to have such a resounding impact on this world was because of his compassionate love, his wish to help and protect all sentient beings throughout the universe. Because of his continual aspiration, this capacity eventually arose. For the same reason, unfathomable buddha activities are able to manifest.

Where does this all-embracing compassionate love come from? It originates with perfect knowledge. There are different kinds of love. Some kinds of love are really just attachment and clinging. Some kinds of love are mistaken love; for instance, through mistaken love one may give weapons to children or irresponsible people. Though they may want such things, they will only harm themselves and others.

6 — Abilities

The root text says that buddhahood possesses 'knowledge, compassionate love, and ability.' Love and compassion are founded on knowledge. Ability is based on compassion.

If buddhahood were not endowed with perfect abilities, the inexhaustible capacity to aid sentient beings, how could the three qualities which benefit others arise? For example, if a mother without arms were to see her infant being carried away by a river, though she has great love for the child, she would lack the ability to rescue it from drowning. Likewise, if buddhahood were lacking the extraordinary capacity to help others, how could it benefit the countless sentient beings?

This perfect quality of enlightened abilities should be long-lasting, all-encompassing, and have great potency. Although Buddha Shakyamuni lived on earth approximately twenty-five hundred years ago, at present innumerable beings still practice his teachings and attain enlightenment. This illustrates the enduring effects of the capacity of buddhahood. Due to the all-encompassing aspect of Lord Buddha's abilities, the Dharma teachings have flourished for thousands of years and become widespread throughout the world. From the vantage point of personal experience, we can see that the Dharma has been disseminated throughout the human realm, yet the Buddha continually emanates bodhisattvas who spread the teachings in places beyond our limited perception. From this standpoint, the enlightened capacity is indeed far-reaching.

To illustrate the strength of the abilities of buddhahood, Lord Buddha was able to spread the teachings over a tremendously vast area without using any physical exertion. Nowadays, communism is propagated worldwide by means of dispatching large numbers of soldiers. Enormous financial expenditures are used to influence other countries to embrace communism. Through the use of weapons, one can easily enforce a particular viewpoint, but the Buddha carried only a begging bowl. Except for his bowl, he is depicted empty-handed. He did not resort to armies or nuclear weapons, but still he had a tremendous impact on the world. This is due to the great strength of the capacity of buddhahood.

Altogether, the Uttara Tantra text lists eight qualities which become manifest at the time of attaining buddhahood, but in short, these can be condensed into just two. When we have realized the profound import of these two aspects of buddhahood, the three perfect qualities which benefit oneself and the three perfect qualities which benefit others, we will feel the need to practice and achieve complete enlightenment as soon as possible.

Questions and Answers

STUDENT: Rinpoche said that the Third Turning of the Wheel of Dharma points out that emptiness is not a mere state of blankness. Does this mean that by practicing the teachings of the Second Turning, one will attain a state of blankness, or is this just a misconception that beginners might have?

RINPOCHE: One does not fall into a blank, mindless state by practicing the Second Turning of the Wheel of Dharma. By meditating on emptiness, the clarity aspect will automatically grow. But in the Third Turning of the Wheel of Dharma, the clarity aspect is emphasized from the very beginning. Therefore, it is said to be swifter. For example, we don't immediately earn the degree of Ph. D. by learning our ABC's, right? Still, we have to start out with ABC.

STUDENT: It was said that Maitreya is a tenth level bodhisattva, why not a thirteenth level?

RINPOCHE: There are two systems: *Sutra and Tantra.* Although there is no great difference between the two, still there is a slight difference in terminology. According to the Sutra system, there are ten bodhisattva levels or 'bhumis.' At the eleventh bhumi, one attains complete enlightenment, whereas, in the tantric teachings, thirteen levels are taught. The eleventh bhumi is called Universal Illumination, the twelfth Lotus of Nonattachment, and the thirteenth bhumi constitutes complete enlightenment. It is called the level of Vajra-holder. One could also say that Maitreya had attained the thirteenth bhumi. It's all the same. Because this teaching belongs to Mahayana, the system of ten bodhisattva levels is used.

STUDENT: But you just said that the thirteenth level is the attainment of enlightenment...

RINPOCHE: According to Vajrayana, it's the state of *Vajradhara,* complete enlightenment.

STUDENT: If the thirteenth level is complete buddhahood, then why is it called a 'bhumi' at all? 'Bhumi' sounds like it's still a stage along the path.

RINPOCHE: The word 'bhumi' in Tibetan is *sa* which means 'level,' 'earth,' 'ground,' or actually 'basis.' In this world, everything takes

26

place on the ground or on the earth, itself. It's the foundation where things can occur. Likewise, the ten bhumis are like the ten foundations for the virtues of bodhisattvas to arise. Westerners usually regard 13 as an unlucky number... [Laughter] so maybe it's better to just speak of ten.

STUDENT: I was wondering if you could say what the enlightened nature is empty of?

RINPOCHE: When we say 'empty,' we usually mean 'without any concrete substance or matter.' When I strike the table with my hand, it makes a sound. That means it has some substance or concreteness. But the enlightened nature, the buddha nature, has no concrete substance whatsoever. It's essence is empty.

When we practice, we should look into the mind wondering, "How is the mind? What is it like?" Our mind gives rise to an inconceivable number of different thoughts and emotions. Most of what we see around us are constructs fabricated by the mind, but still when we sit down and look into the mind asking ourselves, "Where is my mind?" we discover that it is impossible to find anywhere. There's not a 'thing' to be seen or found. That's why it is said that the essence is empty, but is it only empty? No, it's not. Its nature is luminous. Clarity and wakefulness are present because it is possible to know, perceive, and think. At the final stages of enlightenment, inconceivably great virtues and wisdoms manifest.

STUDENT: So, when Karmapa Rangjung Dorje says that it's empty, is he trying to emphasize that even those qualities that appear in the sugata-essence, such as permanence, purity, and so on, are merely our labels and conceptions of it and that ultimately the sugata-essence transcends any words we might apply to it? Is that the force of Rangjung Dorje's argument?

RINPOCHE: Actually, these aspects of being empty, luminous, and having certain qualities are completely interrelated, totally connected. When we say that the sugata-essence has the qualities of purity, permanence, bliss, supreme identity and so forth, it is precisely because its essence is empty that it is permanent, blissful, and so on. Therefore, when we say that the essence is empty, it doesn't mean there is no essence.

STUDENT: In answer to the previous question, Rinpoche said that most of what we see are constructs of the mind. Is it most of what we see, or all of what we see?

RINPOCHE: There are different ways of dealing with this question. For example, the Mind-only school states that everything is made by mind while some proponents say that all experiences or perceptions are made by mind. Take, for example, the stupa outside. It first appeared because someone had the idea, "I should construct a stupa." This is a good example. As a bad example, someone thought, "I ought to make a nuclear bomb." So it seems as though mostly everything is made by mind. [Laughter] But not many people say, "I ought to construct a world."

STUDENT: But what is happening this moment between Rinpoche as the subject and the stupa as the object? Is he creating a mere construct of mind or is the stupa appearing from its own side?

RINPOCHE: There's a difference between a mental experience, or perception, and a mental construct. Right now, we're talking about constructs, not just perceptions.

STUDENT: How does one know when one's experience of emptiness isn't just an intellectual construct?

RINPOCHE: First of all, ordinary beings who have not yet reached the first bodhisattva level are unable to truly perceive emptiness. What we have now is a conceptual understanding of emptiness arising from reasoning, discrimination, and so forth. We have an idea of emptiness.

For example, when looking at a hand, ordinary people have the immediate idea, "This is a hand." They don't have the immediate perception of emptiness. If they use reasoning or discrimination, then they can see that a hand is only *called* 'hand,' though it's actually composed of many things like fingers, skin, flesh, bones, and blood. To this conglomeration, the label 'hand' is appended. Analyzing like this, one can reach the conclusion that the hand is actually empty, but, at present, this is still just an idea. However, as one continues to practice, one grows closer and closer to the actual perception of emptiness.

STUDENT: The qualities of emptiness are spoken of as inseparable: the unity of emptiness and bliss, emptiness and compassion, emptiness and luminosity. Although all the qualities are present, does one realize them individually? Might you realize the unity of emptiness and clarity before you fully realize the compassion aspect, according to your particular obscurations?

RINPOCHE: The qualities of emptiness usually refer to *knowledge, compassion, and abilities.* These occur simultaneously. The degree to which these qualities are manifest depends upon how thoroughly the obscurations have been purified. As obscurations are purified more and more, the enlightened qualities become increasingly manifest. When realizing emptiness, nonconceptual compassion arises spontaneously. When regarding other sentient beings who have not understood emptiness, one feels compassion that they are confused and ignorant.

STUDENT: I thought the Third Turning was the Vajrayana vehicle.

RINPOCHE: The final set of teachings, the Third Turning of the Wheel of Dharma, is entirely connected to Vajrayana in that emphasis is placed on the wisdom or clarity aspect. In Vajrayana practices, such as the *development* and *completion* stages, the main focus is meditation on the clarity or wisdom aspect. Therefore, they are connected. The Third Turning of the Wheel of Dharma is the foundation shared between Sutra and Tantra. The Sutra teachings place greater emphasis on the *prajna or knowledge* aspect. Through discrimination and investigation, one determines the true condition of things. But, in Vajrayana, the *upaya* or *means* is stressed. One is introduced directly to the real condition and then rests in meditation on that.

The Sutra teachings are more extroverted, looking outwardly, examining things, and discriminating while the Vajrayana, or tantric teachings introduce the empty essence and luminous nature directly after which one simply rests in that. Method is of utmost importance and, therefore, Vajrayana is very beneficial and very fast. The link between these two is called the view of the link between Sutra and Tantra.

STUDENT: In Vajrayana, we are introduced to the real condition, the empty and luminous nature. But yesterday Rinpoche said that one cannot experience emptiness until reaching the first bodhisattva bhumi. To me, it sounds like there's a contradiction there.

RINPOCHE: There's no contradiction between the two. It's just a difference in approach. In Sutra, there are *five paths*. On the first path, the path of accumulation, one establishes an understanding of the real condition through learning, reflection, and meditation. On the path of joining, one practices by means of analytical meditation. Finally, one reaches the path of seeing which corresponds to the attainment of the first bodhisattva bhumi. At this point, one directly and fully perceives the truth of dharmata, reality.

The Vajrayana path is slightly different in that from the very starting point one is directly introduced to and recognizes the truth of dharmata, but one's recognition is neither stable nor long-lasting. One is not accustomed to it. Yet, if one practices with great diligence, after being introduced to the view in Vajrayana, one can quickly attain the first bodhisattva bhumi. The very instant of recognizing, the first glimpse, is the truth of dharmata, the innate nature, but it's not the same as the first bodhisattva level because it's not very clear yet, not stable and one is not used to it.

TRANSLATOR: What is meant by the statement that buddhahood is not realized through external causes?

RINPOCHE: There are two different contexts. One context is from the standpoint of the path of ordinary people and the other is from the standpoint of buddhahood, itself. In the former, we are referring to an ordinary person on the path who definitely needs the support of a teacher. The latter refers to the principle of buddhahood, itself, which is independent of external agents. Buddhahood is the manifestation of one's inherent qualities. If it were dependent upon something else for its realization, it wouldn't be perfect buddhahood. It is not something bestowed by one's master. Because of the circumstance of interacting with a qualified master, one can realize one's own enlightened essence, but the teacher, himself, is not the cause of one attaining or not attaining buddhahood.

Here, the text is explaining things from the viewpoint of buddhahood. To make it simple, at present we must rely on the teacher, but once we begin to progress through the bodhisattva bhumis, we don't have to do this. We can actualize buddhahood ourselves.

STUDENT: If love is present, does it necessarily follow that wisdom is also present?

RINPOCHE: There are many kinds of love. There's the love that a mother has for her child, there's the love that family members have for each other, and there's the love which an enlightened buddha has for all sentient beings. They are all 'love', but it doesn't necessarily follow that they all possess perfect knowledge.

STUDENT: Does an arhat possess perfect knowledge?

RINPOCHE: A Hinayana saint does not have the same knowledge or wisdom as a fully enlightened buddha. Only the state of complete buddhahood has perfect knowledge, omniscience. Therefore, the love expressed by an arhat or by ordinary sentient beings cannot be compared with the love and compassion arising from perfect knowledge.

Ordinary people have some degree of wisdom. We can study and learn things, but it doesn't follow that we love all sentient beings and have the capacity to help them. Often, it's the case that a lot of learning and intellectual knowledge produces pride, conceit, and ill-will towards others. It doesn't follow that knowledge produces love, as in the case of buddhahood. In the enlightened state, everything is perceived and completely understood, particularly the condition of others, the nature of their suffering, and what activities are needed to free them from that suffering.

STUDENT: The text says that our motivation to practice should be to attain enlightenment for the benefit of others. We start with love which is the cause for the attainment of enlightenment, but here Rinpoche takes the stand that enlightenment itself is the cause for love. Can Rinpoche clarify this?

RINPOCHE: When speaking of the three qualities of buddhahood: knowledge, love, and ability, the text says that love is based on knowledge, on *seeing,* and that capacity is based on this love. But when we speak in the context of ourselves, who are trainees, then there is no special structure. Sometimes we develop insight based on love and bodhichitta. Sometimes, due to our understanding of things as they are, we feel spontaneous love for others. These qualities don't have to manifest in any particular order.

STUDENT: Will Maitreya realize enlightenment independently?

RINPOCHE: When the bodhisattva Maitreya attains complete enlightenment in the future, it will not depend upon his doing a certain meditation or receiving a certain teaching. Through his own capacity, he will manifest true and complete enlightenment. It doesn't depend upon any additional external instruction. That's why it is said that buddhahood is realized without depending upon external causes.

STUDENT: And in the case of the Buddha, himself?

RINPOCHE: In the Buddha's life, he just acted as though he were receiving instructions from certain teachers, and as though he was learning how to calm the mind. But it was definitely not necessary for him to rely on such teachers in order to attain complete enlightenment. It was just a show, a display. According to Mahayana, the deeds that Lord Buddha performed, such as following the two shamatha teachers, practicing austerity, and so forth were only performances designed to instruct other people. They are not part of his twelve deeds.

STUDENT: I have people coming to my house saying they're enlightened or they attained enlightenment when they were 16. [Laughter] They constantly come around to bother me. What can I do to discourage this?

RINPOCHE: Try hitting them with a stick. First hit them with a stick and if they don't get angry, then they probably are enlightened. [Laughter]

STUDENT: I have heard that when Shakyamuni Buddha first gave the teachings on buddha nature the teachings were considered too profound to be taught and so were kept in a hidden lineage, not among human beings. It was not released into the human realm until Maitreya taught Asanga many centuries later. I was wondering, do you feel we should take this to be literally true, or is it just metaphorical?

RINPOCHE: Take it literally. Don't interpret it as either expedient or ultimate truth. In fact, it needn't be interpreted in any particular way at all.

Lord Buddha gave three sets of teachings which are called the *Three Turnings of the Wheel of Dharma*. These teachings differed slightly to suit the various capacities of different people. Moreover, as an effect of his spontaneously present buddha activity, these teachings were not spread at exactly the same time because the different views and practices would have caused too much confusion in the minds of beings. Instead, teachings were given and practiced in a natural progression. First, for a certain period of time all the teachings and practices focused on the Hinayana viewpoint of reality. At a later date, great masters appeared, such as Nagarjuna who expounded mostly about shunyata and Asanga who revealed teachings about the buddha nature. These two renowned teachers did not appear at the same time, but one after the other. Later on, more emphasis was placed on Vajrayana teachings. The most suitable teachings arise in accordance with the needs and capacity of the beings to be taught. That Dharma teachings appear in their various forms at different time periods to suit the recipients is all due to the activity of the Buddha.

STUDENT: What is the difference between the refuge as the cause and the refuge as the fruition?

RINPOCHE: The difference between the refuge as cause and the refuge as fruition is that when we start on the path we take the Buddha as the example, the Dharma as the path, and the sangha as our companions. That is exactly what is meant by taking the refuge as cause, the causal refuge. Whereas, the refuge of fruition refers to our own attainment of enlightenment, our own future buddhahood which we are aiming at and which we will ultimately attain.

STUDENT: Would you explain that in terms of the path? If you see the refuge as fruition...

TRANSLATOR: That refers to your own attainment of enlightenment in the future.

STUDENT: And you see that as path?

RINPOCHE: The refuge as cause is from the Mahayana point of view. But there is something else to consider. When we have been introduced to the mind essence and have practiced that in our meditation sessions, the essence of that is identical with the fruition, itself. While on the path, that is a reflection of the fruition.

Dharma

The Sanskrit word for 'teachings' is *Dharma*. The word 'dharma' itself has numerous meanings, but we should not confine ourselves to only its literal meaning. In the context of our treatise, there is 'Dharma' and 'non-dharma.' 'Non-dharma' refers to that which harms oneself and others — an unwholesome attitude, negative behavior, and so forth. 'Dharma' conveys just the opposite — that which is true, beneficial, and wholesome. The sacred Dharma refers to the path Lord Buddha has shown. Following this path, we can attain complete enlightenment.

The sacred Dharma falls into two categories:

— the Dharma of Statements;
— the Dharma of Realization.

The Dharma of Statements

The Dharma of Statements pertains to the teachings the Buddha gave after he attained complete enlightenment. With great exactitude, he described the methods and path leading to the fruition — buddhahood. These statements — the words of the Buddha — have been carefully preserved and passed down from person to person until the present day.

The Dharma of Statements has two divisions:

— the words of the Buddha: teachings given by the
    Buddha himself;

> — the *shastras*: treatises given in order to clarify and
> unravel the intended meaning of the Buddha's
> words.

Three different sets of teachings which can be categorized according to discipline, concentration, and knowledge *(shila, samadhi, and prajna)* were given directly by the Buddha. The teachings emphasizing discipline are called *Vinaya;* the teachings emphasizing knowledge are called *Abhidharma;* and the teachings emphasizing concentration are called *Sutra.* These three sets of teachings are collectively known as the *Tripitaka* — the Three Collections.

Treatises are also divided into two groups. The first group of treatises spring from the Indian commentators who are often referred to as the Six Ornaments and the Two Supreme Ones (Nagarjuna and Asanga). This division also includes works authored by the eighty-four mahasiddhas, the eight siddha masters, and numerous other learned masters. The second group of treatises derives from Tibetan authors from all the eight major traditions.

The various themes of Lord Buddha's teachings exist in little bits and pieces. When these have been gathered together and structured into a single body of teachings, the collection is called a treatise which assembles scattered parts. In some cases, the words of the Buddha contained a hidden meaning. The treatise then clarified the hidden meaning, and made it more apparent. This second kind of treatise is called a treatise which reveals concealment. In addition, some of the teachings are very profound and not readily understandable. Therefore, the third kind of treatise, a treatise which opens up profoundness, discloses secret teachings and clarifies them.

When we take refuge, we conceive of the Dharma as a path. First, we study the Dharma of Statements and then we begin to put into practice the Dharma of Realization. In doing so, the refuge becomes the cause of our attaining enlightenment. 'Dharma' in the context of the Uttara Tantra includes both the Dharma of Statements and the Dharma of Realization. However, just as the refuge of fruition is the main focal point in the Uttara Tantra, rather than the refuge of cause, the Dharma of Realization is the principal issue of our text.

The Dharma of Realization has two aspects:

> — the truth of cessation;
> — the truth of the path.

When dust falls on a table, it sticks to the surface and falls no further. In the same way, we have been unable to attain enlightenment because we are in bondage — 'stuck.' That which is free from any kind of bondage is called the truth of cessation. That which frees one from bondage is called the truth of the path.

We practice the Dharma of Realization during both the path and the attainment. Since this is our ultimate goal as well as the means of attaining it, the Uttara Tantra stresses the refuge of fruition. The Dharma of Realization operates according to the law of cause and effect. The cause is the truth of the path, the effect is the truth of cessation. Usually, we begin with an explanation of the cause and then examine the effect, but here it is reversed. We start with the truth of cessation and then ask ourselves, "How can we attain that?" The answer is, "By following the path."

The Dharma of Realization has six qualities:

— three qualities of the truth of cessation;
— three qualities of the truth of the path.

The Qualities of the Truth of Cessation

— inconceivable;
— nondual;
— nonconceptual.

In order to attain the truth of cessation, we must abandon our fixation on concepts. Once this has been accomplished, one realizes the state of cessation of conceptual thinking. How is that characterized? From the point of view of ordinary people, the truth of cessation lies beyond the scope of ordinary thought and is therefore said to be inconceivable. The state of cessation implies that one has truly actualized the enlightened essence, the potential for buddhahood which is the unity of emptiness and luminosity.

Since we are ordinary people, the true meaning of buddha nature and emptiness are beyond our intellectual grasp. How then can we understand what emptiness refers to? At first, we believe that people, mountains, houses, fire, and water are just what they appear to be. People are people, houses are houses, mountains are mountains, long things are long, short things are short, tall is tall, and small is small.

inconceivable

We hold that these things are real and truly exist just as they are. (Rinpoche holds up two sticks, one longer than the other). For example, we can see that one stick is longer than the other. We can ask anyone we meet, "Which stick is longer?" and they will easily make the right choice. They would never say that the shorter stick is longer or the longer stick is shorter. (Rinpoche puts down the short stick and holds up a third stick longer than the long one.) Now, the stick we just labelled as 'longer' is suddenly 'shorter'. All such labels as 'long' or 'short' are just our own invention and the truth of such labelling depends solely upon what the particular entity is being compared to. Compared to our ring finger, our fifth finger is labelled 'short,' but compared to our middle finger, our ring finger is judged 'short.' All concepts are merely a system of labels invented by our conceptual mind. Phenomena do not actually possess any of these characteristics in themselves. In this way, all things are empty of characteristics, empty of being big or small, empty of being long or short.

(Rinpoche waves his hand in the air.) If I say, "This is my hand," when you look at it you will think, "That's right. It's his hand." A hand can be used for many things. I can use it for moving articles from the left side of the table to the right side. We are accustomed to the idea that this object is just a hand. But is the thumb the hand? No, it is not. It is the thumb which is simply composed of two or three joints and a nail. Is the index finger the hand? No, it is not. Similarly, we can ask the same question about each finger. Is the skin the hand? No, it is not. It is the skin. The hand is made up of bones, flesh, blood, and so forth. If we remove these parts and ask, "Where is the hand?" then nothing remains to point to and say, "This is the hand." The mind imputes the idea, "This is my hand," when it sees all these parts together. Following this same logic, everything can be reduced to emptiness.

Now we might ask, "Does that mean that everything is nonexistent or empty like space?" No, it doesn't mean that. Although empty, we can still see the hand and it functions in that capacity. We can call this object a 'hand,' and we can move it and use it. Traditionally, Buddhism utilizes an analogy using the 'horns of a rabbit.' Obviously, a rabbit does not have horns. So if we ask, "Are all things nonexistent like the horns of a rabbit?" we must reply, "No, they are not because objects appear and can be experienced through the five senses." Although the true condition of all things is emptiness, they are not merely empty; by nature, they are also luminous. In this context, 'luminosity' is the potential for phenomena to manifest and be experienced. Because things are a unity of being both empty and luminous, empty and yet arising dependently, this unity is said to be inconceivable. For this reason, the text says that the Dharma is *inconceivable*.

The second quality of the Dharma is *nonduality*. Usually, sentient beings hold tightly to dualistic concepts, such as an 'inner mind' that perceives and an 'external object' that is perceived. Because of this habitual pattern of thinking, when contemplating the teaching we decide that there is something called 'emptiness' and something else called 'luminosity.' Yet, these characteristics cannot possibly exist anywhere as two separate things. Therefore, the enlightened essence is the indivisibility of these two attributes. For this reason, the Dharma is said to be nondual.

The third quality of the Dharma which falls under the truth of cessation is that it is nonconceptual, devoid of thoughts. Sometimes, we have many different kinds of thoughts — proud thoughts, desirous thoughts, good thoughts, and evil thoughts. We have different ways of conceptualizing, but such thoughts do not exist in the empty nature itself. Even at our present stage of development, it is already possible for us to understand this absence of thought, the nonconceptual quality.

For example, we might become angry at someone and experience a very intense feeling that the object of our anger is real. We think, "I really dislike that person. I want to say something awful to him. Maybe I'll start a court case against him." We feel the situation is very real, that a valid event is taking place. However, instead of facing the object of anger, we should look inside and ask, "What is it within myself that is angry? Where is the essence of this anger? Where is it arising from? Is it coming from my heart or my head?" If we try to discover where the angry thought exists, it is impossible to locate anywhere. Likewise, all of our other deluded thoughts, such as likes and dislikes, jealousy, pride, and so forth have no true existence anywhere. As long as we remain focused on the external object, it appears to be truly existent and actually occurring, but when we look within then the thinker becomes like a breeze or movement of air in space. That is the analogy. Although it feels as though something is moving or happening, there is nothing to be found anywhere.

These qualities of Dharma describe the realization of the nature of things. They pertain to the realization of the true nature of reality — what is fact. The state of fruition, the result, arises from that realization.

Furthermore, we already possess the truth of cessation, but it is not yet actualized. In order to actualize this, we need the truth of the path.

The Qualities of the Truth of the Path

— purity;
— clarity;
— remedial power.

The path is the antidote which eliminates the two kinds of obscurations — the obscuration of disturbing emotions and the obscuration of dualistic knowledge — thoughts and negative emotions which are in direct contradiction to the nature of how things are. In this respect, the path is called the *remedial power*. We will begin by explaining this third quality.

The obscuration of disturbing emotions is more widely known as the three basic poisons or as the expanded version of five poisons — attachment, aggression, delusion, pride, and jealousy. They are called 'poisons' because if we eat poison, we will die. As long as we harbor these poisons in our mind-stream, we will never find happiness and others will not enjoy our company.

The obscuration of dualistic knowledge is, for example, to look at one's hand and think, "This is a hand." Such dualistic thinking is not harmful in itself, yet it obscures the perception of how things truly are. The path remedies these two obscurations. This 'remedy' has two additional qualities: purity because it is not tainted by any force or cause, and clarity, a kind of trust and confidence.

In brief, these attributes of the path — purity, clarity, and remedial power — are like the sun. The sun is pure and clear because it creates daylight, and it is the perfect antidote to darkness. Likewise, the truth of the path is pure, clear, and the very antidote to obscurations.

Questions and Answers

STUDENT: I would like to know the difference between ignorance as one of the five poisons and the obscuration of dualistic knowledge.

RINPOCHE: In the sense of being ignorant, or mistaken, they are identical. However, there is a slight difference. The obscuration of dualistic knowledge is not necessarily the cause of samsara. It is just the inability to see reality. It is never defined as a cause for further existence in samsara. Whereas, ignorance has two aspects: not knowing why one may suddenly feel strong desire or anger plus thinking that the object of the anger or desire truly exists. Therefore, ignorance coexists with the anger and furthers samsaric existence.

STUDENT: Is it possible to experience ignorance without it being attached to one of the five poisons?

RINPOCHE: There are two kinds of ignorance — mixed and unmixed. In short, 'mixed ignorance' is mixed with negative emotions. But it is possible to have ignorance without any negative emotion. 'Unmixed ignorance' is the lack of direct knowledge of reality.

STUDENT: I don't see why ignorance alone is not the cause of samsara.

RINPOCHE: Of the two kinds of obscurations, when the obscuration of disturbing emotions has been purified one attains the state of an arhat — one is liberated from samsara. Nevertheless, an arhat has not yet purified the obscuration of dualistic knowledge. There is still some fixation and for that reason complete enlightenment has not been achieved.

STUDENT: Where is everything taking place? In the body or the mind or where?

RINPOCHE: Although everything is empty, phenomena is not, like the horns of a rabbit, nonexistent. There is luminosity, or manifestation. Everything can occur; events unfold all the time. Because of that, we begin to fixate and cling to wrong ideas. That is the inception of ignorance.

STUDENT: So where does it come from?

RINPOCHE: It comes from *dharmadhatu*, the reality of things. Because of the union of emptiness and luminosity, there is the potential for

41

things to take place. For that very reason, we give rise to ignorance and make mistakes. That is where the confusion comes from.

STUDENT: How is nonduality related to luminosity?

RINPOCHE: It is said that in their basic condition, things are empty in essence and luminous in nature. These are not two separate entities. Essence and nature are undivided, so it is called nondual.

Sangha

As explained in the previous chapter, refuge has two aspects: the *refuge of cause* and the *refuge of fruition*. In our text, *sangha* should be understood as part of the 'refuge of fruition' and not the sangha we visualize when taking refuge or doing prostrations.

Sangha as the Refuge of Cause

In general, the term *sangha of causal refuge* refers to our companions on the path, those following Buddha Shakyamuni's teachings. Because he lived twenty-five centuries ago, at present we cannot meet the Buddha in person and receive his teachings directly. We cannot know what he actually said and did. However, the Buddha established a *noble sangha* which has continued in an unbroken succession throughout the ages until this present day. Thus, the sacred teachings have been perfectly preserved. We can consider the noble sangha our companions on the path because they are skilled in helping us practice what is unfamiliar. When we are unable to practice due to, say, laziness, the noble sangha give us encouragement and urge us along the path. This is called the sangha of causal refuge.

Sangha as the Refuge of Fruition

The Uttara Tantra depicts the sangha as the *refuge of fruition*. In the previous chapters, both the sacred Dharma and buddhahood, itself, were said to have eight qualities. The sangha also has eight qualities.

In Tibetan, the basic qualities of the sangha of fruition are called *rig-dröl* meaning 'knowledge' and 'liberation.' You could say this term *rig-dröl* has almost the same meaning as buddha or bodhi.

'Buddha' is *sangye* in Tibetan. *Sang* means 'purified.' When complete buddhahood is attained, the obscurations or defects have been completely cast away. *Gye* means the qualities of buddhahood have been 'fully developed,' unfolded.

The Sanskrit word *bodhi* translates as *Jangchub* in Tibetan. *Jang* means that which should be abandoned has been 'purified' and *chub* refers to the 'perfection' of the wisdom and qualities of enlightenment.

Rig means 'perfect knowledge,' realization, and *dröl* refers to one's 'liberation' from that which should be abandoned. So the meaning is almost the same as bodhi. However, buddhahood refers to the final result and therein lies the difference. Enlightenment — bodhi — expresses a more gradual accomplishment. Knowledge and liberation — rig dröl — is incomplete because one hasn't quite attained the final result yet.

Indian commentaries on the Uttara Tantra describe the sangha as possessing only four qualities, but Tibetan masters assert four additional qualities, making eight altogether.

The qualities of knowledge:

1 — The wisdom of knowing the nature as it is,
2 — The wisdom of seeing all that exists, and
3 — The perception of inner wisdom.

1 — The Wisdom of Knowing the Nature as it is

In general Dharma terminology, the *wisdom of knowing the nature as it is* refers to the profound knowledge of the absolute while the *wisdom of seeing all that exists* refers to the all-encompassing knowledge of the relative nature of things, perceiving whatever appears in accordance with causation, with dependent arising. In short, the first kind of wisdom perceives the empty aspect of things, the profound ultimate truth, the very nature of reality. The second kind of wisdom perceives the extensive relative truth.

In Tibetan, *jitawa*, means 'exactly as it is.' For example, seeing red as red, black as black, big as big, and small as small. If we see red as black, or small as big, and so forth we are, of course, not perceiving things as they are. The wisdom of knowing the nature as it is simply means perceiving the nature of phenomena exactly as it is. With this knowledge, the noble sangha truly perceives the nature of reality. Usually, things are perceived as naturally solid, having real substantial existence. But a member of the noble sangha perceives the world as it truly is, having no true, concrete existence. The real condition of things is perceived as empty in essence and luminous in nature.

2 — The Wisdom of Seeing All that Exists

In Tibetan, *jinyepa* means 'whatever exists' or 'all that is.' It is a term used in the context of these two wisdom qualities. Literally, it means if there are three objects, one perceives three objects; if there are one hundred objects, one sees all one hundred. One perceives whatever exists, all that exists, not partially, but completely. All things in the world, whatever their characteristics or qualities, are known exactly as they are. It is a complete understanding. An ordinary person's knowledge may be extensive, yet it has definite limits beyond which the intellect cannot reach. But a member of the noble sangha possesses an all-encompassing knowledge.

3 — The Perception of Inner Wisdom

The third quality of knowledge is called the perception of inner wisdom. This means that one perceives the potential for enlightenment within oneself, the sugata-essence, the basic nature of buddhahood within each sentient being. This perception of inner wisdom is the understanding that all sentient beings, as well as oneself, are capable of attaining complete enlightenment. Based on this third kind of wisdom, one will not fall into despair or become discouraged, thinking, "I can never attain enlightenment," or "I'm unable to accomplish the benefit of beings." This special wisdom perceives that one already has the seed, the cause for enlightenment, buddhahood. Therefore, one should also have the capacity to accomplish the welfare of beings since they possess this enlightened potential, too. They are just as ready to attain enlightenment, so there is certainly no basis for feeling discouraged.

Because sentient beings have different dispositions and varying capacities, it seems as though one will only be able to help some and not others. What is appropriate for some beings might not be suitable for others. It may even seem as though some beings have the potential for enlightenment and others have not, but this is definitely not the case. All sentient beings, without exception, possess the enlightened essence, the potential for buddhahood. Some beings are more intelligent than others, some have faith and trust while others have none, but still all possess the enlightened essence. Because of having the enlightened essence, even those without much intelligence or trust are able to develop.

Though he knows it will take many aeons, a great bodhisattva is never overwhelmed at the prospect of benefiting countless sentient beings. He doesn't become discouraged, thinking, "If it takes one or two aeons, I'll be able to help these beings, but if it takes more than that, it will be impossible. There are too many sentient beings." Because of this third quality, the perception of inner wisdom, bodhisattvas have the courage and fearlessness to endeavor in their vast activities.

It is said that these three types of knowledge are utterly pure. This utter purity of the three qualities of knowledge leads to the three qualities of liberation.

The Three Qualities of Liberation

1 — Freedom from bondage — to be free from
    defilements;
2 — Freedom from obstruction — the impediment to
    knowledge;
3 — Freedom from inferior views — the attitudes of the
    shravakas and pratyekabuddhas.

These three kinds of freedom are called liberation.

1 — Freedom from Bondage

The first quality of liberation is called freedom from bondage. In some contexts, 'bondage' is identical with attachment or desire, but here it refers to the bondage of the obscuration of all disturbing emotions because the three poisons of attachment, aggression, and delusion bind us to samsara.

2 — Freedom from Obstruction

The second quality of liberation is called freedom from obstruction. Here, 'obstruction' refers to an impediment to knowledge, our inability to perceive the nature of reality. When we are obstructed by a wall, we are unable to see what's on the other side or go through it. Likewise, at present, we are unable to perceive the actual nature of things.

3 — Freedom from Inferior Views

The third kind of knowledge, the perception of inner wisdom, is actually included within the first two wisdoms, the wisdom of knowing the nature as it is and the wisdom of seeing whatever exists, but to further clarify and emphasize the importance of the perception of inner wisdom, it is described as a separate quality. Likewise, the third quality of liberation, the freedom from the obscuration of clinging to the inferior view of shravakas and pratyekabuddhas, is actually included within the first two qualities, freedom from the bondage of disturbing emotions and freedom from the obstruction of dualistic knowledge. However, to emphasize the importance of the bodhisattva's selfless attitude, as opposed to the shravaka and pratyekabuddha's attitude, it is described as a separate quality.

The shravaka is not concerned with other sentient beings' potential for buddhahood and therefore does not feel inclined to even attempt to benefit other beings. The pratyekabuddha feels it is sufficient to attain enlightenment merely for himself and, for this reason, has no wish to benefit others. Actually, such attitudes are the antithesis of the perception of inner wisdom and, in fact, the only antidote is the perception of inner wisdom.

In summary, sangha members endowed with these unexcelled virtues or wisdom qualities are called noble sangha and are beyond returning to samsara. They possess the two basic qualities of knowledge and liberation. When these two attributes are elaborated upon, each has three additional aspects. In the Tibetan mode of counting, these six plus the two main qualities add up to eight.

Questions and Answers

STUDENT: Would Rinpoche say something further about the obscurations and how they relate to the six *paramitas?*

RINPOCHE: The six paramitas nullify the obscuration of disturbing emotions. For example, transcendent generosity abolishes stinginess or greed. Discipline disallows frivolous behavior which is often caused by attachment or aversion. Patience overcomes anger. Diligence cancels out laziness. Reflection remedies the fault of distraction and transcendent knowledge dispels distorted perception.

STUDENT: How do ordinary beings and buddhas differ in their perceptions?

RINPOCHE: The everyday knowledge that we sentient beings have at present and the knowledge that bodhisattvas possess is, in essence, identical. However, there's a difference in the quality of perception. Our knowledge is based on deduction, or inference, and our understanding is, therefore, more conceptual. For example, when studying something, we get an idea of what the material is about, but it is not a direct understanding. Yet, once we reach the first bodhisattva bhumi, our knowledge and understanding becomes direct, not inferential. At present, we have a very gross, superficial grasp of how things are. Bodhisattvas possess a more penetrating knowledge of reality. But still it's essentially the same knowledge.

Nevertheless, until he or she reaches complete enlightenment, the bodhisattva's knowledge is also imperfect. They must still mingle meditation and post-meditation periods. In meditation periods, their knowledge is insight into *dharmata,* itself, but during post-meditation periods their knowledge can still be momentarily obscured by impure perceptions. Later on, when complete enlightenment is realized, meditation and post-meditation periods have completely intermingled so that while a buddha perceives 'others' or is teaching, his mind never departs from the natural state.

At the time of attaining complete enlightenment, there are two acquisitions: the wisdom of seeing the nature as it is and the wisdom of seeing all that is. In the perception of the buddhas, nothing whatsoever exists inherently; not even sentient beings. 'Things' only exist according to the distorted perception of the sentient beings. Because the buddhas have a perfect knowledge of all things that exist in the conventional sense, they know what sentient beings experience and that sentient beings suffer as a result of their confused perceptions. Although the buddhas, themselves, have realized that suffering has no inherent existence, still they manifest very great non-conceptual compassion for beings who perceive suffering as real. Nevertheless, it's also possible that the Enlightened Ones perceive all living beings as divine and perfect because the Uttara Tantra states that all sentient beings possess the enlightened essence. There's actually no contradiction in that.

STUDENT: I don't quite understand the difference between ultimate and relative bodhichitta.

RINPOCHE: When we start out on the path, we aim for *absolute bodhichitta*; we turn our attention in that direction. Therefore, our intention, itself, is called *relative bodhichitta*. Absolute, or ultimate, bodhichitta pertains to the direct realization of reality, dharmata. *Bodhi* refers to enlightenment. *Chitta* refers to the mind. Together they imply direct insight into the true nature of reality.

STUDENT: What is meant by the *blessing of the lama?*

RINPOCHE: Blessings are not concrete entities which pass from one pot to another. There's no such thing. Nonetheless, if we have openness and trust, then we develop a certain capacity which corresponds to whomever we have faith in. If we have complete trust in the guru, then we have the genuine capacity to accomplish whatever he or she has accomplished. That is what blessing actually means. While practicing on the path, devotion is very important because it is the teacher who shows us *how* to practice. To practice, we must have confidence in what we are doing. Otherwise, the practice will not be very effective. If we think, "Maybe this will achieve a perfect result and maybe not," then we are uncertain about what we're doing. This kind of doubt makes it impossible to attain a final fruition. If we have only 50% trust in what we're doing, we'll only get a half-hearted result. In order to feel genuine confidence in our practice, we need to trust the source of the teaching; in other words, we must have complete confidence in our teacher. Therefore, devotion is essential.

Buddha Nature

As followers of Gampopa, Dakpo Rinpoche, we should follow his advice. He said that a practitioner should engage himself in study, reflection, and meditation all at the same time; in other words, while we study we should also practice. How does that relate to our present situation? We should regard this teaching as an instruction in how to practice.

The Four Inconceivable Vajra Points

4 — Buddha Nature;
5 — Enlightenment;
6 — Enlightened Qualities;
7 — Buddha Activity.

After having explained the meaning of the Three Jewels from the *Uttara Tantra*, which form the first three of the Inconceivable Vajra Points and are quite easy to understand, we will now continue with the fourth vajra point which concerns the enlightened essence, the potential for buddhahood.

Why are all sentient beings endowed with the enlightened essence? A four-line verse appears in the *Uttara Tantra* listing three reasons why all sentient beings are never apart from the buddha nature:

(Because the body of complete buddhahood is all-
pervasive,

> Because the suchness is indivisible,
> And because of possessing the potential,
> All beings constantly have the buddha essence.

Other religions and belief systems describe the final fruition of practice as the attainment of something new which arises from some other source. In Buddhism, this is not the case. Because dharmakaya is all-pervasive, the end result of complete enlightenment is already present within oneself. The bodies of complete enlightenment, *dharmakaya, sambhogakaya*, and *nirmanakaya* originate from oneself and not from any place outside. When attaining enlightenment, these two latter bodies are manifested from dharmakaya.

Right now, we may doubt the possibility of someday possessing the same vast enlightened capacity and unfathomable qualities as Buddha Shakyamuni, but since we do, in fact, possess the same enlightened essence, when evolving the body of complete enlightenment we will automatically manifest all of these wondrous attributes.

Next, *suchness is indivisible.* There is no difference whatsoever between the suchness, or *dharmadhatu* nature, that is present at the time of complete enlightenment and the suchness that we possess at this moment. In essence, they are identical. The suchness of fully enlightened buddhas and the suchness of ordinary beings, like ourselves, is exactly the same. If the suchness of complete enlightenment were very exalted and the suchness of sentient beings were inferior, it would then appear as though we lacked the sugata-essence, the buddha nature, but this is not the case. There is not the slightest difference. Hence, the qualities which will manifest at the time of reaching complete enlightenment are spontaneously present within oneself right now.

Finally, each sentient being naturally possesses this enlightened potential. Of any hundred beings, all one hundred have the potential for enlightenment. We cannot say that only ninety-five of the hundred will attain enlightenment while the remaining five have no chance, no matter how hard they try. Each and every being has this potential for enlightenment. These three reasons explain why all sentient beings are endowed with the enlightened essence.

It is crucial to acknowledge what we naturally possess. Why? In terms of Dharma, the major obstacles to practice and accomplishments are laziness and discouraging oneself. 'Discouragement' includes putting oneself down, thinking, "I can't practice. People like Milarepa can attain enlightenment, but someone like me has no such capacity. I'll never become enlightened." Instead of discouraging ourselves, we should remember that Buddha Shakyamuni attained enlightenment because he possessed the sugata-essence. Milarepa also attained complete liberation due to the enlightened essence. Because we have this same buddha nature, we are absolutely identical to them in our ability to attain enlightenment. Regardless of whether we are rich or poor, male or female, educated or uneducated, we are capable of practicing the Dharma and attaining liberation. In this respect, we are all the same.

In an ordinary worldly context, people sometimes discourage themselves saying, "I can't get a job. I don't know what to do. I wish I were dead," and they may even consider suicide. This happens. Nevertheless, if people would acknowledge their potential for accumulating enlightened merit, they could then tap this immense capacity to discover new ways of living. Therefore, understanding that we have the enlightened essence as our natural possession is extremely important and beneficial both for this present life, future lives, and for the attainment of the ultimate fruition, complete liberation and perfect buddhahood.

When the Buddha taught that sentient beings possess the sugata-essence, it was not solely for the purpose of encouraging us to practice. He was simply stating the truth. Through understanding our real condition, how things truly are, we can then develop the perseverance and fortitude to complete our journey along the path.

Buddha Nature

The ten ways of describing the buddha nature are:

1 — The Principle;
2 — The Cause;
3 — The Fruition;
4 — The Function;
5 — The Endowments;
6 — The Manifestation;
7 — The Phases;
8 — All-pervasiveness;
9 — Changelessness;
10 — Indivisibility.

1 — The Principle

The first point is called the principle. To help us understand the principle of an undefiled buddha nature, Lord Maitreya used three metaphors: a gemstone, space, and water. He explained that although these can be temporarily tainted, or stained, their intrinsic nature always remains pure, with no defects whatsoever.

Normally, gemstones are found deep in the earth and when excavated are often encrusted with soil. Yet, the jewel itself is pure within and untainted by the temporary mud stains.

Sometimes the sky is veiled by clouds, mist, or smog and to those on the ground it appears obscured, but space itself remains essentially pure and untouched. Likewise, although at present the negative emotions obscure our enlightened essence, it remains naturally pure and immaculate.

Finally, if water is mixed with soil, it becomes dense and murky, but this is not an irreversible state. The water and dirt haven't fused into an inseparable mixture and the water can always be purified, again. The water itself remains essentially pristine. In the same way, although the buddha nature is now concealed by gross and subtle defilements, these can be purified so that one's natural, unspoiled condition emerges.

At first glance, these three analogies seem quite similar, but this treatise was taught by a very exalted being, Lord Maitreya, so each example actually has a slightly different connotation.

The example of the gem means that, although presently encrusted with stains, when it is washed clean the stone's very special qualities are instantly revealed.

Why is space used as an example? On one hand, the analogy that space remains untainted by clouds is very similar to that of the gemstone, but, on the other hand, space represents that which is changeless. From the moment of the world's creation until now, space has remained forever unchanged. Likewise, the sugata-essence is our unchanging buddha nature.

Why is water used as an analogy for the enlightened essence? Water is wet and makes things develop and grow. It nurtures flowers, plants, and so forth. In the same way, the enlightened essence is saturated with compassion which cultivates the welfare of both oneself and others. The enlightened essence has natural qualities as beneficial as the life-sustaining element, water.

Therefore, in principle, the enlightened essence is:

— Intrinsically pure and untainted by the temporary
  defilements,
— Full of qualities and capabilities,
— Changeless,
— Saturated with compassionate love.

2 — The Cause

There are four causes that purify the defilements which obscure the enlightened essence:

1 — Devotion or interest in the Dharma,
2 — Discriminating knowledge, prajna,
3 — Concentration,
4 — Compassion.

There are four reasons why our enlightened essence has remained dormant; hence, we need four causes in order to actualize it. The first reason why we have been unable to realize the enlightened essence is that we feel either uninterested or hostile towards Dharma teachings and have, therefore, been disinclined to practice. Once we engender interest and devotion in the Dharma, our hesitation and dislike will vanish. We will then be able to practice and realize our true condition.

Although we may feel devotion and be interested in the Dharma, without abandoning ego-clinging we will be unable to realize the enlightened essence. Ego-clinging, the belief in a self, is the basis for all disturbing emotions. As long as we retain this fixation on a self, these emotions will continue to plague us. Without giving up disturbing emotions, we cannot escape cyclic existence. The remedy for the belief in a self is *prajna,* the discriminating knowledge of the real condition of things. Once we develop prajna, the understanding of egolessness, we will be able to cut through ego-clinging, undermine the causes for samsara, and realize our innate buddha nature.

Ego-clinging sometimes arises based on our attitude toward the physical body. We think, "This body is me." Sometimes ego-clinging is based on our attitude toward the mind, thinking, "This mind is me." We think of our belongings, clothes, and dwelling place as 'mine.' Yet, the belief in a self or ego-clinging arises due to our initial mistake and the ensuing confusion. For example, when a friend has a nice wristwatch we never think, "This is my watch." We know it belongs to another person and if it should fall on the ground and break, we think "His watch broke," but we don't feel particularly upset about it. If he had given it to us, we would think, "This watch belongs to me," and if it were to break we would say, "Oh no, my watch broke!" We would feel unhappy. This misery is created by ego-clinging. The wristwatch itself doesn't care who owns it. A watch is just a watch. When ego-clinging has been abandoned, suffering will automatically disappear and the watch will be understood to be just what it is — a watch.

Furthermore, although we fear the suffering of samsara and want to be liberated from it, the causes for attaining enlightenment are yet incomplete. We need one additional cause: the special concentration called *samadhi*. Due to the bliss and inherent qualities of samadhi, when we generate this special concentration our fear of samsaric misery vanishes.

We may indeed possess the three previous causes for enlightenment, however, when we are careless and indifferent towards sentient beings, thinking, "If I become enlightened that will be enough. I don't care what happens to the others," then the conditions for attaining complete enlightenment are not truly present. Compassion is an essential cause. Through compassion, we give rise to the wish to accomplish the welfare of all sentient beings. With this special motivation, the causes are complete for our attainment of enlightenment.

3 — The Fruition

The third point, fruition, possesses four transcendent qualities:

— transcendent purity;
— transcendent identity;
— transcendent bliss;
— transcendent permanence.

These four transcendent qualities: purity, identity, bliss, and permanence describe the fruition of having realized the buddha nature.

Transcendent purity refers to the natural purity of the enlightened essence itself. When the enlightened essence is realized as the dharmakaya, the quality of purity emerges because both the two obscurations and the habitual patterns that perpetuate them have been totally purified.

Because sentient beings harbor the notion of a self, an ego, the Buddha gave teachings on the lack of a self-entity. Nonetheless, since the ego has never had any true existence to start with, in reality, how can something called 'egolessness' have any true existence? The second quality, *transcendent identity*, refers not only to the total pacification of one's artificial mental fabrication of a 'self', but also to the pacification of one's intellectual concepts about egolessness — that of individuals and that of things. This complete pacification reveals one's true identity. Mental constructs of self and non-self are completely absent in both the enlightened essence and at the time of realizing the dharmakaya. Therefore, when conceptualizations about self and non-self are totally pacified the true identity is unveiled.

Usually, ordinary sentient beings caught in samsaric existence cling to their feelings. Although these feelings are nothing but the three kinds of suffering, sentient beings perceive them as happiness. Therefore, the Buddha taught the truth of suffering as well as its cause, the origin: the five aggregates, disturbing emotions, and misdeeds. Because the very nature of the five conditioned aggregates is misery, as long as one possesses the five aggregates the opportunity for achieving perfect, lasting happiness is forever absent.

Recognizing suffering as suffering, Hinayana practitioners — shravakas and pratyekabuddhas — develop strong renunciation and the wish to escape and be liberated from cyclic existence. However, when one realizes the enlightened essence, the state of dharmakaya beyond both suffering and happiness, one has thus abandoned the truth of suffering along with its cause — the disturbing emotions, misdeeds, the five subtle aggregates as well as the five gross aggregates, and one's subtle habitual patterns. Therefore, the third transcendent quality of *transcendent bliss* and happiness is also realized.

The fourth transcendent quality is permanence. Although the Buddha taught the truth of impermanence in order to dispel our clinging to the permanence of transient objects, when the fruition of the path is actualized one realizes the sameness of samsara and nirvana — both are essentially non-existent. Having no concrete existence, this nature is not worsened by samsara nor improved by nirvana. The unchanging realization of this 'sameness of nature' constitutes the fourth quality — *transcendent permanence*.

4 — The Function

The fourth of the ten points describes the function of the enlightened essence. Because the enlightened essence is naturally endowed with wisdom and intelligence, sentient beings are able to feel revulsion for the sufferings of samsara and engender the strong desire for freedom. This recurring dissatisfaction with cyclic existence is due to the influence and function of the enlightened essence.

5 — The Endowments

Traditionally, two analogies are used to describe the enlightened essence and its qualities, or endowments: at the time of the ground, the starting point, the enlightened essence and its endowments are likened to a gem-filled ocean while at the time of fruition, when the dharmakaya is realized, the enlightened essence and its qualities are likened to the flame of a butter lamp.

Like a vast ocean filled with precious gemstones, at the time of the ground the enlightened essence possesses immense, inconceivable qualities such as the wisdom of the victorious ones, the buddhas. In addition, an ocean resembles a great vessel which holds vast amounts of water. In the same way, the enlightened essence, or dharmakaya, is the basis, or support, for all the qualities of the buddhas. Moreover, just as the nature of water is wetness, the enlightened essence is naturally moistened with boundless compassion for all sentient beings.

At the time of fruition, the enlightened essence manifests three special qualities which are inseparable from the essence itself:

— flawlessness;
— clarity;
— indivisibility.

These three attributes can be likened to the flame of a butter lamp whose essence is light and whose nature is clear and bright. These two facets, the luminosity and its clarity, are indivisible.

Returning to the enlightened essence, the quality of 'flawlessness' describes the immaculate, untainted wisdom of all the buddhas. The quality of 'clarity' denotes the brilliance of higher perceptions, such as clairvoyance and so forth, with which the enlightened essence, the dharmakaya, is endowed. Thirdly, the quality of 'indivisibility,' implies that the first two factors, flawlessness and clarity, are inseparable.

6 — Gradual Involvement

Gradual involvement means the enlightened essence endures continuously so that sentient beings gradually attain realization. When the enlightened essence is polluted or obscured, one is called an ordinary being. Later, when it is half-purified, the ordinary being has become a bodhisattva. Later still, when the enlightened essence is completely freed from all impurities, the bodhisattva has become a buddha. It's a gradual procedure.

7 — The Phases

The enlightened essence is revealed through three different phases, or stages. These phases do not imply three different modes of the enlightened essence itself, but allude to the degree to which we have, through practice, purified and cleared away the various kinds of gross and subtle obscurations, such as the *obscuration of disturbing emotions* and the *obscuration of dualistic knowledge*. The three phases describe the conditions whereby the obscurations are not yet purified, partially purified, and totally purified.

In terms of the *five paths,* at the time of entering the path of seeing, all mental imputations — the gross obscuration of disturbing emotions and the gross obscuration of dualistic knowledge — have been purified and abandoned. When reaching the path of cultivation, the subtle innate obscurations have been purified and relinquished. The *imputed* aspect of the obscuration of disturbing emotions is not something we are born with. Adopting a particular belief system or philosophy, one attaches certain attributes to phenomena which are not truly present. One may embrace a philosophical system which imputes the existence of a self-entity in consciousness or a self-entity in matter. For example, one may assert the existence of a personality who is creating everything or believe in a real self located somewhere. This imputed aspect of the obscuration of disturbing emotions is cleared away when one realizes selflessness. Disturbing emotions are

59

based on the belief in a self, in ego-clinging. Once ego-clinging is cast away, disturbing emotions automatically disappear.

The *inherent* aspect of the obscuration of disturbing emotions is not created by a certain belief or philosophical system that one adopts. It is the product of our intrinsic ego-clinging and the disturbing emotions arising therefrom. All sentient beings are born with this innate or coemergent ignorance. We automatically think, 'I am.' This, itself, is the inherent aspect.

The imputed aspect of the obscuration of dualistic knowledge is, for example, believing that everything is created by God or Mahadeva. This is a gross general concept which contradicts the nature of things. This *imputed ignorance* is purified when one realizes that all things lack self-entity and are naturally empty. Since the imputed aspect of the obscuration of dualistic knowledge is more easy to abandon, it is already purified at the path of seeing.

The *inherent* aspect of the obscuration of dualistic knowledge is the belief in the self-existence of a perceiving subject and perceived objects. For example, upon seeing an object, we automatically believe that the object truly exists from its own side, independently. We also believe that the perceiving mind truly exists from its own side. Furthermore, we assert the existence of a physical body in-between. These ideas do not have to be developed or fabricated in anyway whatsoever. They are an automatic expression of past habits which have been enforced since beginningless time. Even a tiny infant has this inherent obscuration. It's another form of 'coemergent ignorance.'

The imputed aspects of the obscurations can be abandoned all at once, but the inherent aspects are shed at a more gradual rate. First the coarse, then the more subtle, and finally the most subtle delusions are progressively cleared away.

Merely perceiving the nature of reality, *dharmata,* is not sufficient to purify these inherent obscurations because the habits of mistaken perception are very powerful. Since beginningless time, we have perpetuated these errors. One must become accustomed to perceiving the true nature of reality again and again. The term "cultivation" in the phrase "path of cultivation" pertains to getting used to how things truly are. During this time, the subtle inherent obscurations are permanently cast away.

Right now, both the imputed and the inherent obscurations are 'discards' that should be abandoned at the time of entering the path of seeing and the path of cultivation. At present, as ordinary people, we have not relinquished these two obscurations. Although we have entered the Dharma, we have not completed the path of seeing or the path of cultivation. Because these obscurations are not yet cleared away, this stage is called the phase wherein the enlightened essence is not purified.

When entering the path of seeing, one directly perceives the truth of reality. In the case of a shravaka, or Hinayana practitioner, only the obscuration of the disturbing emotions in the imputed aspect has been purified upon entering the path of seeing. In the case of a bodhisattva, both the imputed aspects of the obscuration of disturbing emotions as well as the imputed aspects of the obscuration of dualistic knowledge have been abandoned upon entering the path of seeing.

The second phase of the enlightened essence is called the pure/impure stage. A bodhisattva on the first bhumi, called the Joyous, has purified all the imputed aspects of the obscurations simultaneously, but the inherent aspects have not yet been cleared away. Since the imputed aspects are purified, this phase is called the pure stage, but because the inherent aspects are not yet cleared away it is also called the impure stage. As one progresses through the bhumis all the inherent obscurations, from gross to subtle, are gradually purified. Nonetheless, from the first bhumi through the tenth bhumi inherent obscurations must be continually purified. Therefore, this stage is referred to as the phase of the pure/impure enlightened essence.

When one attains complete enlightenment, all the gross and subtle obscurations of disturbing emotions and of dualistic knowledge are utterly purified, without the slightest residue. Therefore, this stage is called the phase of total purity.

Since the buddha nature has three phases, three different names are ascribed to it. During the first phase, when the two obscurations have not been purified, the enlightened essence is called 'sentient being.' Later on, when the imputed aspects of the obscurations are purified, but the inherent aspects are not, the enlightened essence is called 'bodhisattva.' Finally, when all obscurations are totally purified, the enlightened essence is called 'buddha.'

When we are taught that the buddha nature remains essentially the same during the three phases of existence: as a sentient being, a bodhisattva, or a fully enlightened buddha, there is danger that we might think it is identical with what non-Buddhists call the 'true self' or what the Mind-only school calls *alaya*. Be careful to avoid these misconceptions.

In the days of Taranatha of the Jonangpa School, other learned masters made numerous objections to his presentation of the buddha nature, but not because they perceived a defect in Taranatha's view and wanted to refute it. The other masters feared that practitioners might misunderstand the correct view and make a grave error. Attempts to avoid that danger triggered a great deal of debate.

Much debate arose among those who regarded the enlightened essence as identical with what in the Samkhya Hindu system is called the 'true self' or the 'conscious self'. According to many non-Buddhists, the 'true self' is a permanent, concrete, independent entity. However, being the unity of space and wisdom, or *dharmadhatu* and primordial wakefulness, the enlightened essence is naturally empty in itself. Therefore, it can never be equated with the characteristics of a true self as posited by the Samkhya school.

Likewise, although the buddha nature bears some resemblance to the *alaya* asserted by the adherents of the Mind-only school, the alaya is not considered empty in essence. It is considered concrete and real. The enlightened essence is the unity of space and wisdom and its essence is empty. Hence, how can the alaya and the enlightened essence be the same?

8 — All-pervasiveness

The enlightened essence is all-pervasive. The example for this is space. Space permeates everywhere. It even permeates seemingly solid objects, like the stupa in Boudhanath. Even lowly places, like toilets, are permeated by space. High or low, pure or impure, everything is penetrated by space. Likewise, regardless of whether a sentient being is high or low, pure or impure, all beings are pervaded by the enlightened essence.

9 — Changelessness

The ninth vajra point can be explained in many different ways. It refers to the *changelessness* of the enlightened essence. Whether obscured or whether purified of obscurations, the buddha nature remains forever unchanged. Yet, previously we asserted three phases of existence. How can the Buddha nature manifest in three stages if it remains essentially changeless? The enlightened essence itself never changes, but the obscurations that veil it do change and, therefore, can be completely eliminated. Because the disturbing emotions that conceal the buddha nature are momentary and fleeting, like clouds in the sky, they can be cleared away. Sometimes the sky is obscured by clouds and sometimes the sky is clear. Clouds are momentary and temporary, but the sky itself has always existed naturally. In the same way, because disturbing emotions are momentary and not inherent to the enlightened essence they can definitely be vanquished.

Space permeates all things. Within the expanse of space, whole universes are formed, destroyed, and again come into being, yet space itself neither arises nor ceases. Likewise, the enlightened essence permeates all sentient beings. Although the beings themselves undergo many different kinds of change, like suffering, happiness, birth, old age, sickness, and finally death, no change occurs in the buddha nature itself. Constant change manifests only on the level of what sentient beings experience. The sugata-essence remains ever changeless.

Though the enlightened essence remains immutable while one is an ordinary person, does any modification arise when one becomes a bodhisattva? The answer is no. It is generally agreed that the sugata-essence is changeless when one is an ordinary sentient being, changeless when one becomes a bodhisattva, and changeless when one attains complete enlightenment.

Our text states that the sons of the Victorious Ones, bodhisattvas who have realized the nature as it is and have seen the truth of suchness, of *dharmata,* have thereby transcended birth, old age, sickness, and death. Nevertheless, due to their great compassion for sentient beings, bodhisattvas still behave as though they experience these aspects of cyclic existence. Noble beings do not actually undergo the miseries of birth, old age, sickness, and death because these events are created by karmas and the obscuration of disturbing emotions. In order to become a noble being in the first place, these karmas and disturbing emotions must have been abandoned whereupon the tribulations of samsara are no longer endured. Nevertheless, bodhisattvas take on the guise of the class of beings among whom they appear; in other words, they manifest as ordinary beings who are obscured by ignorance and undergo suffering.

Just as bodhisattvas feign birth, old age, sickness, and death in order to benefit sentient beings, the fully enlightened Buddha also manifested such events in his life on earth. However, he did not really undergo these things; they were merely the display of his compassion.

The fact that bodhisattvas seem to behave like sentient beings is a great marvel. The perfectly enlightened Buddha Shakyamuni appeared to take birth, become a householder, and subsequently a king. Later on, it appeared as though he abandoned everything, took ordination, and finally blessed his disciples and passed away. But this is not what really happened. He displayed these events so that human beings could perceive this drama. In truth, nothing could have prevented the Buddha from flying down from the sky, landing among the flowers, emitting light-rays, and so forth. He would have had no problem doing such things, but other beings would then have thought the Buddha was not really human. They would have thought, "How could we ever attain enlightenment?" Therefore, the Buddha appeared to take birth from a mother's womb.

Buddha Shakyamuni could have begun by acting out the role of a monk or a great bodhisattva, but ordinary people would have become discouraged. To avoid this, the Buddha became a householder, married, and ruled his kingdom for a number of years. Later, he abandoned his domain and became a monk. If he hadn't done that, again ordinary people would have thought, "The Buddha is already a great being. We can never be like him." Therefore, he began by emulating the ordinary way of life and afterwards acted as though entering the Dharma path. This behavior is called 'acting in accordance with the behavior of a class of beings.'

It would have been entirely possible for the Buddha to live for one hundred, five hundred, or five thousand years without passing away, but human beings don't live that long. If Buddha Shakyamuni had not conformed with the normal life span of his day, people would have said, "He's not an ordinary human being like us. We can only live for 70 or 80 years so we can't possibly attain what he has attained." Therefore, in accordance with ordinary beings, the Buddha passed away at about 80 years of age.

Some people become a little doubtful, or suspicious, and wonder why a very great master like His Holiness Karmapa developed cancer and passed away or why Dudjom Rinpoche was frequently ill. It's not bad to have these doubts; in fact, it's actually good.

As explained in the text, bodhisattvas and buddhas behave as though undergoing old age, sickness, and death to accord with the expectations of ordinary beings. If they didn't do this, we would think these masters are completely unlike ourselves and impossible to emulate. Therefore, because some people contract cancer, some masters also display cancer symptoms. Because some people are constantly ill, some masters act as though sick all the time.

The Hinayana scriptures state that the Buddha was offered a meal of cold pork which made him ill and subsequently caused his death. Nonetheless, the sutras translated into Tibetan assert that, after eating his last meal, the Buddha displayed the act of passing away into nirvana. These two stories seem contradictory, but it is entirely possible that the Buddha just acted as though eating a meal of cold pork, acted as though it made him ill, and acted as though passing away into nirvana.

Bodhisattvas and buddhas are completely free from the taints of any defects whatsoever. Buddhahood itself is free from birth, old age, sickness, and death. As a result, it possesses four qualities.

Buddhahood is:

— steadfast;
— permanent;
— peaceful;
— changeless.

Having fully realized the enlightened essence, buddhahood is permanent because it is free from birth, steadfast because it is free from old age, peaceful because it is free from sickness, and changeless because it is free from death.

10 — Indivisibility

The enlightened essence is inseparable from its qualities. For example, when the sun is free from cloud-cover, it is already there — naturally luminous and shining. After the clouds clear away, we don't have to do anything to make the sun generate its sunlight which we then dispense to the world. That's not the case at all. The sun is inseparable from it's luminous and radiant qualities and emits light rays naturally. In the same way, once the enlightened essence is realized, we don't have to then somehow invent its qualities. They are insepa-rable and spontaneously present so that the very moment the last remnant of obscuration is purified, these qualities manifest automati-cally.

Obscurations as the Nine Analogies

First, we explained three reasons why all sentient beings have the enlightened essence. Next, we examined, through ten items, the manner in which this enlightened essence manifests. Now, we're ready to discuss the nine analogies which depict how the enlightened essence is, at present, hidden by obscurations. The Uttara Tantra ex-plains these points in detail, but we'll just touch on each one briefly.

The first analogy is that of a small buddha statue concealed within a withering lotus flower. As long as it remains hidden by the shriveled petals, we cannot know it is there, yet when the petals are shed the buddha's image is instantly revealed. At present, our own buddha nature is obscured by the veil of disturbing emotions.

The second metaphor is honey. Honey is sweet and delicious to eat, but if the honey is covered with a cluster of bees, it's impossible to even taste it. Nevertheless, once the bees are dispelled we can enjoy the honey's natural goodness.

The next example is a grain of rice. Most people like rice, but when it is covered by the husk, it is inedible. Whether the grain of rice remains within the husk or is extracted, the quality of the grain itself does not suffer in the least. It's still just rice, but for the one who eats it there's a very big difference in whether or not the rice has been husked.

The fourth analogy compares the enlightened essence to a lump of gold covered with dirt. Imagine that a few thousand years ago some-one dropped a big lump of gold into a ditch. Slowly, it became com-pletely encrusted with soil and debris so that no one could see it lay-ing there. The gold itself couldn't call out, "Hey, I'm here! Please take me out and clean me." So, there it stayed. Finally, one day a clairvoy-ant person happened by who could clearly see the gold laying in the ditch. He told people, "Look! There's gold here! Dig it up, wash away the impurities, and use the gold for whatever you like." Likewise, when the enlightened essence is recognized and purified, it is invalu-able. Even unrecognized, it is still priceless.

The fifth example describes a casket of precious gems hidden under the floor in a poor man's house. Though a treasure of jewels lies unseen just beneath his feet, the fellow hasn't realized this and so undergoes the terrible suffering of deprivation. Unless he uncovers this store of wealth, it won't help him at all. Likewise, although all sentient beings possess the enlightened potential, they will continue to undergo needless suffering until the buddha nature is realized.

The seed of a tree comprises the sixth metaphor. Even a tiny seed can grow into a tree many meters high. Despite close examination, we are unable to perceive the potential tree intrinsic to the seed because it isn't actualized yet. Nonetheless, the seed definitely possesses this latent capacity. Similarly, many qualities lie dormant within the enlightened essence, yet at present they are not actualized.

The seventh example describes the image of a buddha wrapped in old rags and therefore undetectable. Our enlightened essence is, in the same way, temporarily obscured by defilements so that we are unable to recognize it.

Eighth is the example of a destitute woman who carries in her womb a child destined to become a great king. The woman is completely impoverished and living under difficult conditions, perhaps even sick. She has no enjoyments whatsoever. Yet, she carries a child who will later become a great ruler. At this time, no one knows of her unseen possession. Even she herself is unaware. In just this way, all sentient beings 'carry' within them the enlightened essence which need only be realized. Though now imperceptible, when this essence is realized and fully actualized, the buddha qualities will be immediately evident.

Lastly, the sugata-essence can be likened to a complete buddha statue which, though perfectly cast, remains yet within the mold. According to the age-old tradition, a statue of wax is melted away within a clay mold before pouring the gold inside. Later, the mold is broken and the golden statue removed. However, in our example, the mold hasn't been removed yet. This precious statue is made of pure gold and, having just the right proportions, is exquisite to behold. Nevertheless, since the rough clay mold still envelops it, we cannot discern the beautiful statue within. Likewise, shrouded by obscurations, the enlightened essence is imperceptible to ordinary sentient beings.

Obviously, the general meaning of all nine examples is that the enlightened essence is obscured by defilement. Therefore, we may think, "Why are so many examples given if there's only a single idea to comprehend?" But each of the nine examples has a particular inner message and illustrates a definite point. Let's look at these examples, again.

First, we are told the enlightened essence is similar to a statue of the buddha concealed within a wilting lotus blossom. A fresh lotus flower is very appealing to the eye, but as the days go by the flower loses its freshness and grows less and less attractive. By the third or fourth day, the petals begin to dry out and fall off. Likewise, at first the object of our desire seems fascinating yet, as time passes, sooner or later the fascination wears off. The withering lotus is used to illustrate the defilement of desire because attachment clouds the sugata-essence.

The example of the bees portrays the buddha nature masked by aggression. The honey itself is sweet and delicious, but bees are easily irritated. When angered, they sting and cause suffering. Likewise, anger or aggression hurts one's own mind and brings suffering to others.

The example of rice within the husk symbolizes ignorance. Rice is an important staple. It sustains beings, keeping them alive and nourished. But if the rice remains enveloped by a very hard and unpleasant husk, it is inedible and therefore useless. Like grain encased by husk, sentient beings are totally enveloped by ignorance, unknowing.

Defilements can either be latent or manifest. The fourth example, a lump of gold embedded in filth, represents manifest defilements. The manifest defilements of attachment, aggression, stupidity, and so forth constitute impurities that obstruct our perception of the enlightened essence.

Latent defilements are quite dense and also completely obscure our perception of the buddha nature. The fifth example depicts riches buried under one's house. Though it would be easy to reach such a treasure, the earth is dense and one is unable to detect anything hidden below ground. In the same way, though easy to purify, our latent defilements are quite dense and obscuring.

Previously, we mentioned 'that which is abandoned when attaining the path of seeing' and 'that which is abandoned when attaining the path of cultivation.'

Once a seed is planted, it naturally grows into a tree. In the same way, once the wisdom of the path of seeing has taken birth within oneself, defilements and obscurations are naturally cast away.

Ragged clothes concealing a lovely buddha image are easily stripped away. Likewise, that which is to be abandoned at the path of cultivation is very easily discarded.

The eighth and ninth examples describe a nation's ruler still within his mother's womb and a magnificent statue still within its clay mold. Yet in time this future king, who already exists as an embryo, will take birth; the statue, already finished and perfect, will be gradually freed of its encasement.

The first seven of the ten bodhisattvas levels are called the *seven impure bhumis* while the last three are termed the *three pure bhumis.* The first seven are called 'impure' because some ego-clinging lingers whereas ego-clinging has been totally purified upon reaching the three highest levels.

Why Were Teachings Given on Buddha Nature?

Buddha Shakyamuni began his Dharma teachings in Varanasi. There, for the first time, he taught the Four Noble Truths:

— the truth of suffering;
— the truth of the origin of suffering;
— the truth of cessation;
— the truth of the path.

These teachings comprise the First Turning of the Wheel of Dharma.

At that time, the Buddha explained that every action has its effect, or result. He taught about the suffering of cyclic existence and disclosed the cause of this suffering. He also prescribed a path to be followed and described the cessation to be realized.

Later, the Buddha journeyed to Vulture's Peak at Rajgir and other places expounding what is called the intermediate teachings — the Second Turning of the Wheel of Dharma which explains emptiness, the absence of characteristics. He taught that, although things appear, they have no true existence whatsoever. He compared the world of cyclic existence to a dream, an illusion, a magical display. All phenomena, he said, are as nonexistent as clouds which possess no concreteness whatsoever. He taught the *Heart Sutra,* the *Prajnaparamita in 25,000 Verses,* and so forth which emphasize the emptiness aspect of reality. For instance, the *Heart Sutra* says:

> "There is no eye, no ear, no nose, no tongue..."

Finally, the Buddha gave his ultimate teachings in the Third Turning of the Wheel of Dharma known as the *Total Uncovering* or *Full Discernment.* At that time, he taught that all sentient beings are endowed with the enlightened essence, the buddha nature.

One might give rise to doubt, thinking, "In the Second Turning of the Wheel of Dharma, the Buddha had already taught that all phenomena are nonexistent, like clouds, dreams, and illusions, therefore, how could he suddenly assert the existence of the buddha nature in sentient beings?"

In the First Turning of Wheel of Dharma, the Buddha indeed taught that things exist. In the Second Turning, he then said that things do not truly exist, that all phenomena are empty. Then, at the Third Turning, the Buddha seemed to again contradict himself by asserting the existence of an enlightened essence. Nevertheless, he gave each of these teachings for a specific purpose.

The Buddha began the teachings by expounding the existence of karma: action and its result. If he had started out by saying everything is empty, people would have misunderstood, become irresponsible, and stopped caring about the results of their actions. To avoid this, he first described the effects of karma. However, if one sustains the belief that everything truly exists, it is impossible to realize the *dharma-dhatu* — the empty nature of things.

In order to explain the lack of self-existence of things and of the individual person, the Buddha gave the intermediate set of teachings. If, at that time, the Buddha had taught about the enlightened essence, also called *tathagata-essence,* beings would have been unable to discard the fixation that it is something concrete. They would have mistaken the buddha nature to be a soul or a true self. Teaching about emptiness first — the lack of characteristics of all phenomena — the Buddha made certain this mistake would not occur in people's minds.

Five Reasons for Giving These Teachings

After the truth of twofold selflessness had been properly assimilated, teachings on the enlightened essence were given. There are five reasons why the teachings on the enlightened essence were given to ordinary sentient beings.

The first reason was to counteract discouragement or faintness of heart. We might think, "Great bodhisattvas are brilliant, full of compassion, and extraordinarily diligent. They can easily attain complete enlightenment, but people like me who are not very smart and have little diligence can never attain such a high state. There's not much point in trying." Discouraging oneself in this way, one feels faint-hearted and incapable. To counteract this mistaken belief, we should understand that we have the potential for complete enlightenment, the buddha nature, as our natural possession. Therefore, we need never feel discouraged.

If we develop the mind set on supreme enlightenment, bodhichitta, and accumulate merit, we will be able to follow in the footsteps of the buddhas and bodhisattvas and attain complete enlightenment. Emulating the actions of the great bodhisattvas in our lineage, our kind root gurus, we can attain the same results. We can follow the same path and meditate at the same level of samadhi. Why? Because we possess the same buddha nature. In this respect, there is no difference whatsoever in the quality of the enlightened essence possessed by an ordinary person and that possessed by a great bodhisattva.

The second reason is that we might imagine ourselves to be special bodhisattvas. After practicing for some time, we might think, "I've truly developed bodhichitta. I've progressed on the path with extraordinary courage. My meditation is profound, my compassion sublime. Other sentient beings don't have great courage, bodhichitta, or compassion." If such feelings of pride or superiority cause us to look down upon others, our good qualities will naturally be blocked from manifesting and instead defects will arise.

A Dharma student should think of himself as a vessel into which the master 'pours' the teachings. Yet, compared to a vessel, pride is like a steel ball. When a substance is poured on a steel ball, it rolls right off. Nothing adheres. If one is filled with conceit or pride, one cannot learn or develop any new qualities.

Though we may have developed a few virtues, they are utterly insignificant when compared with the virtues and qualities of completely enlightened beings. Because all sentient beings possess the enlightened essence, although they may not have developed these virtues yet, they are definitely capable of developing qualities to the same extent as oneself; even to a higher degree than oneself! They, too, can attain complete enlightenment. Once we acknowledge the capacity of other beings, we will not disregard or look upon them with disdain.

Thirdly, the enlightened essence was taught because it is necessary that sentient beings abandon what is untrue — i.e. false beliefs. For example, some non-Buddhist belief systems teach that if one performs good deeds either a Supreme Being or a pantheon of deities will be pleased, but if one engages in wicked actions these deities will be angered.

The Buddhist viewpoint differs from this notion. In short, the Buddha taught that when our mind is mistaken, it continually wanders throughout the confusion of cyclic existence. Yet when we realize the nature of things — the real condition — and discard the obscurations, we then free ourselves from samsara.

For example, imagine we are in a dark place and a piece of mottled rope is laying on the ground. Because it is laying in the shadows, we mistake the rope for a poisonous snake. Frightened, we think, "What should I do? Maybe it will bite me! If it's very poisonous, I might die." Our fear increases along with our concepts, but it seems as though we are helpless. We can't eat a pill and make it go away. We can't pray to a divine being, saying, "Please get rid of this snake." However, at that very moment there is one thing we can do to help ourselves — we can examine our real situation. We may need to consult a third party, asking, "Is that really a snake or not?" Checking carefully we will discover it is not truly a snake at all, just a rope. Through seeing what actually is, both our mistake and the resulting confusion are immediately cleared away. At that point, our mind will automatically become relaxed, peaceful, and free from suffering. We have realized the truth.

As this analogy indicates, we are presently wandering in samsara due to the combination of the ripening of our past karma and our confused reactions, the disturbing emotions, to what we experience. Because we are in a deluded state, mistaking all our experiences, we suffer. There is only one solution. We must look into the truth of reality, and discover precisely the nature of things. Most people lack the courage and self-confidence to do that. Therefore, we must rely on the teachings of the Buddha who explained how we can develop the knowledge that perceives the state of egolessness, the ultimate reality. By relying on his words, we will be able to cut through confusion.

The Buddha gave very complete and extensive teachings on the nature of reality. Nothing was withheld. Therefore, once we have understood the correct view — the unity of the Second and Third Turning of the Wheel of Dharma — we will have a complete picture of ultimate reality.

The Second Turning of the Wheel of Dharma emphasizes the empty aspect of phenomena, but this is not equated with a blank or vacant state, like the space around us. If we think emptiness is merely void space, our understanding is incomplete — not the ultimate truth. If we think the enlightened essence has only the quality of wisdom, that is also incomplete. Emptiness is luminous, the very unity of space and wisdom, or wakefulness. This luminous aspect is the main issue in the Third Turning of the Wheel of Dharma.

The fourth reason why this teaching was given was to dispel faults which may arise from failing to understand the entire scope of the Buddha's teachings. Not knowing the teachings in their entirety, one is in danger of developing wrong ideas and doubts concerning the perfect teachings. Understanding the complete message, including the description of the buddha nature in the Third Turning of the Wheel of Dharma, one will not develop faults which might cause one to stray from the true teachings.

The fifth reason for giving this teaching was to vanquish self-cherishing. If we misunderstand the teachings on the enlightened essence, we might begin to think that we are very special and that we should attain enlightenment solely to end our own suffering. However, when we realize that the enlightened essence exists within all sentient beings and that, like ourselves, all these beings must be freed from the obscurations and attain enlightenment, we will feel naturally inclined to discard self-cherishing. The five reasons for giving a teaching about the enlightened essence are solely to help us discard these five defects. For this reason, the Buddha ultimately gave the Third Turning of the Wheel of Dharma on the *Total Uncovering*.

Questions and Answers

STUDENT: I don't understand what *gradual involvement* refers to.

RINPOCHE: Here, 'involvement' describes our involvement in the process of realizing the enlightened essence; turning in the direction of realization. We don't have to get involved in samsaric existence because we already are in samsara.

STUDENT: How is suffering related to the five aggregates?

RINPOCHE: In order to understand why the five aggregates belong to the truth of suffering, you must first understand what 'suffering' means. Suffering can be classified under three headings: first, the *suffering upon suffering* which is the actual experience of misery or pain either in one's body or in one's mind. This is how suffering is often described. However, sometimes we are without physical pain or mental suffering and so we feel temporarily relaxed and happy. Nevertheless, we cannot remain in this state permanently. It always changes. This kind of happiness is transitory and therefore one is subject to the *suffering of change*. Regardless of whether we find ourselves in a state of pleasure or pain or indifference, change will sooner or later arise. Unlike the permanence of the dharmakaya and buddhahood, sentient beings are always subject to transient, impermanent states of existence. This is called the *all-pervasive suffering of formation*.

Each aggregate is subject to the same three kinds of suffering. For example, perception and consciousness — painful perceptions or painful states of mind — are the suffering upon suffering. Pleasant perceptions or states of mind are always prone to change and this is nothing but the suffering of change. Because all of our feelings and states of mind and body are fleeting and transient, they are never beyond the all-pervasive suffering of formation.

STUDENT: In the sense of something to be abandoned, what is meant by 'subtle habits' or 'patterns' in relation to happiness or bliss?

RINPOCHE: A subtle habit is like being used to something for a long time. Even though the stimuli may no longer be present, there still remains a kind of habit related to it. For example, let's say a bottle once contained musk. Even though the musk may have been discarded long ago so that not a trace remains for the eye to see, still

74

some scent will linger. This metaphor resembles someone having attained the state of arhathood. Although manifest disturbing emotions have vanished, still some habitual patterns remain. It is said that, in an instant of distraction, an arhat might accidentally step on a snake. That kind of carelessness is due to the obscuration of habitual patterns which have not been thoroughly purified. Nonetheless, an arhat no longer has the strong disturbing emotions to which ordinary people are subject.

There are different ways of understanding what constitutes realization of the enlightened essence. The enlightened essence has already been realized on the path of seeing, but that is not the attainment of dharmakaya or buddhahood because it is incomplete. The Uttara Tantra uses the example of a precious jewel buried in the ground. At first, it is completely covered with soil. No one can see that it is really a magnificent gemstone, yet with a little washing its qualities become evident. This refers to the attainment of the path of seeing. One's buddha nature is partially realized. Recognizing that something precious is close at hand, it can then be polished until its beauty becomes even more evident. Eventually, it can be fine-polished until it is like a lovely piece of lapis that can be sold or used as an adornment.

In the same way, when the enlightened essence is realized upon the attainment of the path of seeing, some obscurations linger which must be purified. As these are being cleared away more and more, the enlightened essence is thereby gradually more apparent until at the final stage of complete enlightenment, all impurities have vanished.

STUDENT: How are the lineages traced?

RINPOCHE: In terms of the Kagyü lineage, we trace the original source of the teachings back to the Dharmakaya Buddha, Vajradhara, then Tilopa, Naropa, Marpa, Milarepa, Gampopa, and so forth. Tilopa and Buddha Shakyamuni did not live in the same era. Tilopa appeared some years later. So what happened? What is the difference between Vajradhara and Buddha Shakyamuni? Buddha Shakyamuni is called the supreme nirmanakaya. He manifested on this planet, attained complete enlightenment, performed the twelve enlightened deeds and so forth. However, the source, the dharmakaya wisdom-body of Buddha Shakyamuni, was actually inseparable from Vajradhara. In that sense, when Tilopa, through the strength of his enlightened perception, met Vajradhara in person and received the teachings, there was no difference between meeting Vajradhara and meeting Buddha Shakyamuni.

Likewise, according to the Nyingma lineage, the *wisdom-body dharmakaya* of Buddha Shakyamuni is inseparable from the wisdom-body dharmakaya known as Buddha Samantabhadra from whom Garab Dorje received direct transmission.

One of the qualities of buddhahood is spontaneous presence. That means that the influence of buddhahood, the buddha activities, are always in accordance with the capabilities of beings alive at certain periods. The various teachings evolved throughout different historical periods. The Hinayana teachings were mainly in effect from the time of the Buddha up until the days of Dignaga. The Mahayana teachings had their beginnings mainly at the monastic institute, Nalanda, during the time of Asanga and Nagarjuna. Later on, in the days of the Vikramashila Monastery, Vajrayana teachings began to flourish. It is not that the teaching itself changed; through the spontaneously present buddha activity, different teachings became appropriate at different times for the different capabilities of beings.

At present, we have taken advantage of the teachings that were established by Shantarakshita, Trisong Deutsen, and the master Padmasambhava. In general, Tibetan Buddhist teachings are called 'Vajrayana,' yet they are essentially the system of the *Vajra-holder of the Three Precepts*: externally, the *vows of individual liberation;* internally, the *bodhisattva trainings;* and secretly, the *Vajrayana samayas.* All four schools of Tibetan Buddhism, the Geluk, Sakya, Kagyü, and Nyingma, advocate this system of keeping the precepts of all three vehicles simultaneously in whatever practice is undertaken these days.

In the general Dharma teachings, it is said that samsara is phenomena which appear depending upon causes and conditions; therefore, samsara is empty of any self-entity and has no concrete existence. Nirvana, also essentially nonexistent, means 'passing beyond misery.' However, in order to pass beyond the misery of samsara, samsara must truly exist in the first place. Yet, if samsara has no concrete existence, no real being, then nirvana must also have no true existence. Right?

We are, however, describing the buddha nature itself which is never stained by the defilements of samsara nor enhanced by the purity of nirvana. Lord Maitreya likened the sugata-essence to a precious jewel. Regardless of whether it lays in the earth covered with soil or is

excavated, washed, and polished, the jewel itself remains totally unchanged. Its intrinsic nature is not stained by the casing of mud nor
improved by any cleansing process. In the same way, whether obscured by defilements or cleared of these obscurations, the enlightened essence remains inherently pure and untouched. There is no
change in it whatsoever.

Still, for those on the path, there is a big difference between the
'obscured' sugata-essence and the 'unobscured' sugata-essence. But
this difference lies entirely in the obscuration. The buddha nature remains, like a jewel buried in the depths of the earth, totally
unchanged.

According to the Sutra teachings, this is taught through deduction
or inference whereby the student believes in the existence of an enlightened essence which is obscured by defilements. But according to
the *Mahamudra,* or *Dzogchen* teachings within Vajrayana, the buddha nature is taken into actual practice. For example, after having
received the *pointing-out instruction* of Mahamudra or Dzogchen,
one rests in meditation and looks inward. In the moment of recognition, obscurations completely vanish and one comes face to face with
one's true nature, the enlightened essence.

STUDENT: Does the Kagyü school consider the Mind-only school a totally wrong view or is it a partially correct view? Can one attain complete enlightenment through practices of the Mind-only school?

RINPOCHE: The Mind-only system, the shravaka system, and the
pratyekabuddha system suffer from a few defects in their ultimate
viewpoints, but they also possess some good qualities. For this reason,
one will progress slowly when entering the path of any one of these
schools. Despite these shortcomings, one will eventually reach the
higher path later on.

Regarding the Mind-only system, there is nothing whatsoever
wrong with resolving that all phenomenon are mind. But there is
some flaw in believing that the nature of mind has true existence.
Still, it doesn't matter very much because if one continues to practice
according to the beliefs of the Mind-only school, one will purify one's
negative actions.

I have been asked many times, "What is the difference between
belief in the true existence of an enlightened essence and the Mind-
only view that the nature of mind has true existence?" The answer is
that these two are quite different because the enlightened essence is

the unity of wakefulness and space and is, therefore, essentially empty. But this wakefulness is naturally replete with wisdoms, enlightened qualities. Still, it is never claimed that the enlightened essence has any true or concrete existence. Whereas the Mind-only view point holds the nature of mind to have true, concrete existence, that the cognizance of mind truly exists. They say if there were no real cognizance, being conscious, there would be no basis for cognition of things occurring. Therefore, they establish that something truly exists which has the ability to cognize. That contradicts the view of *Madhyamika*. The view of an empty yet wakeful enlightened essence is in accordance with Madhyamika philosophy. However, it is said that the enlightened essence is actually beyond the confines of both existence and non-existence.

In a practical sense, we have to try to talk about it. It seems impractical to say that our topic of discussion doesn't really exist, right? Therefore, we usually say that there exists an enlightened essence, but this doesn't mean that it is not beyond the four complexities.

STUDENT: What is the relationship between the obscuration of dualistic knowledge and the two different ignorances, coemergent ignorance and conceptual ignorance?

RINPOCHE: The *obscuration of dualistic knowledge* refers to holding on to the threefold conceptualization of subject, object, and action. For example, when giving something away, we think, "I am the giver, that person is the receiver, and something is passing between us." Merely holding these three concepts, however subtle, in mind constitutes what is commonly called the obscuration of dualistic knowledge. It obstructs omniscience, insight into the real nature of things. The *obscuration of disturbing emotions* is that which obstructs liberation. Both are a type of ignorance. However, in the case of the obscuration of dualistic knowledge, the ignorance itself is not a cause for samsara. It is somewhat neutral ground because it just means one is holding on to a concept. No disturbing emotions are involved. Therefore, it is called 'unmixed' ignorance.

However, the obscuration of disturbing emotions is called 'mixed' ignorance because it is combined with negative emotions such as attachment, anger, pride, jealousy, and so forth. The two kinds of ignorance described in other talks, innate and imputed or coemergent and conceptual ignorance, don't exactly correspond to this context. *Coemergent ignorance* is intrinsic or primordial ignorance, not knowing the nature of things. *Conceptual ignorance* refers to imputing, or labelling, things with concepts which don't really apply and characteristics which are not truly present. There is a slight difference.

For instance, when looking at a table, the obscuration of dualistic knowledge comes into play merely by our thinking, "This is a table." The idea obstructs our perception or insight into the empty nature of that object. Still, there's nothing particularly negative about just thinking, "It's a table." Whereas, conceptual ignorance is a little more pressing, such as joining a religion that teaches everything is created by God. Agreeing with the other followers, one thinks, "Yes, everything is created by God." From that point on, a whole set of fallacious concepts evolve.

STUDENT: What is the difference between a tulku and Buddha Shakyamuni?

RINPOCHE: Buddha Shakyamuni is called a supreme nirmanakaya, which is actually the sambhogakaya and nirmanakaya manifested in one person who is the embodiment of everything in just one spot. But nowadays, we hear 'tulku this' and 'tulku that.' There are a lot of tulkus around, but it seems to me to be the nirmanakaya without the sambhogakaya.

STUDENT: So, is Rinpoche saying then that we as ordinary beings possess the quality of buddha nature which is obscured, but that it's not a level of nirmanakaya?

RINPOCHE: As long as the enlightened essence has not been realized, the three kayas are not present. They are not present right now.

STUDENT: What is the level of their existence?

RINPOCHE: Right now, we don't possess the three kayas, do we?

STUDENT: I would think, "Yes," because it is said that the essence is always there and always pure, just temporarily obscured. The kayas are simultaneously existing, otherwise that would not be true.

RINPOCHE: Where is your sambhogakaya?

STUDENT: It is obscured.

RINPOCHE: When we use the words *enlightened essence*, it's not the same as *Enlightened One*. In Sanskrit, *tathagata-essence* is not the same as the *Tathagata*, otherwise there would be no reason for using two different terms. 'Essence' refers to qualities which are not yet manifest or realized. It is just like a flower seed. It is called a seed, not called a flower. Nonetheless, the seed has the potential to become a flower if it is planted, but it is not a flower yet.

STUDENT: Well, that goes to the heart of my question. The seed has all the potential, but in terms of fruition, you can't eliminate the development and that development is actually prescribed, is that true?

TRANSLATOR: That is called *path*.

STUDENT: Yes. In other words, there is no such thing as sudden enlightenment. One has to go through that process, including realization of the kayas.

RINPOCHE: The process of development depends entirely upon the individual's capacity. For example, the Mahayana teachings say it takes three great aeons to realize the enlightened essence. Yet according to the Vajrayana path, realization and complete enlightenment can be achieved very rapidly, sometimes within one lifetime, sometimes within just a few lifetimes. There is no fixed time period. We cannot say you will become enlightened right away or that it will take a very long time.

STUDENT: What is the difference between the inherent aspects of the obscuration of disturbing emotions and the inherent aspects of the obscuration of dualistic knowledge?

RINPOCHE: The *inherent obscuration of disturbing emotions* pertains to emotions such as pride, jealousy, anger, and so forth which we naturally possess without our having to cultivate anything. The *inherent obscuration of dualistic knowledge* refers to such ideas as 'I' and 'other' which we naturally have without having to be taught.

STUDENT: Can one abandon all these obscurations on the spot?

RINPOCHE: We cannot say that one cannot abandon them all at once because there is the *sudden path*. However, in general, it is a gradual step-by-step process. Obscurations are very subtle.

STUDENT: It seems that by making contact with the enlightened essence, one can immediately abandon the obscurations.

RINPOCHE: At present, it is not the case that the enlightened essence, even if recognized, is totally free from obscurations. There's a difference between *recognizing, realizing,* and *awakening* to complete and perfect enlightenment. At the first bodhisattva level, the buddha nature is recognized, but it is not totally realized. On the path of cultivation, one's buddha nature is periodically clouded by defilements. Therefore, it's called 'cultivation' because one has to again and again cultivate or become accustomed to the enlightened essence. When all obscurations are finally totally purified, complete enlightenment manifests.

STUDENT: What is the difference between gross and subtle obscurations?. Is 'gross' just evident like anger and the 'subtle' more like a seed which, without the proper environment, lays dormant but with the potential to arise?

RINPOCHE: Yes, it is just like that. Gross defilements are what is present, or manifest. The subtle defilements are not visible and not really manifest, but are categorized into nine divisions which are the very gross defilements, the medium gross, and the subtle gross, the gross medium, the medium medium, and the subtle medium, and so forth. These nine categories correspond to the obscurations purified from the second to the tenth bhumi. Subtle defilements are not manifest, but they are just ready to pop up like a seed that can suddenly sprout. However, there are other seeds which do sprout easily. A lot of conditions must come together before the most subtle obscurations can sprout.

STUDENT: Does the path of cultivation remove the last most subtle obscurations?

RINPOCHE: On the first bodhisattva bhumi, the imputed very gross defilements are purified and cast away. All the other nine steps belong to the path of cultivation.

Enlightenment

The fifth vajra topic concerns realization of the enlightened essence. Therefore, we will now describe the enlightened essence when freed of all defilements at the time of complete realization.

Enlightenment can be explained under eight points:

1 — The Nature;
2 — The Cause;
3 — The Fruition;
4 — The Function;
5 — The Endowments;
6 — The Manifestation;
7 — Permanence;
8 — Inconceivability.

1 — The Nature

This first point describes two qualities:

— perfect abandonment;
— perfect realization.

Because the nature of the enlightened essence is clarity, or luminosity, it is likened to the sun and sky. On a cloudy day, the sky seems hazy and unclear and even the sun itself is hidden. Yet the moment the clouds blow away, a dazzling sun is revealed shining in the ever-pure blue sky. Likewise, though the enlightened essence is present and already endowed with all the qualities of perfect abandonment and perfect realization, these qualities are camouflaged by the obscuration of disturbing emotions and the obscuration of dualistic knowledge. Hence, the qualities are not manifest and even the enlightened essence itself, veiled by these fleeting obscurations, remains unrecognized. However, when we enter the *five paths*, progress through the seven impure bodhisattva bhumis and then the three pure bhumis, and finally purify the final obscurations through the *vajra-like samadhi*, the enlightened essence will be totally unveiled and its qualities will immediately be apparent. This is known as the complete enlightenment of buddhahood.

Enlightened qualities are permanent, everlasting, and unchanging. Defilements are ephemeral. After they are removed, can they reoccur? No, they will never reappear. Earlier, we mentioned the analogy of mistaking a length of rope for a snake. At first, one imagines the rope is a poisonous snake, but having picked up and examined it, one discovers that the 'snake' is just a rope. Afterwards, no matter how many times one sees the piece of rope, one will never again mistake it for a snake. In the same way, once we have achieved genuine insight into *dharmata*, we will never again be mistaken about the nature of reality.

2 — The Cause

What is the cause for attaining the state of enlightenment endowed with permanent, everlasting, and unchanging qualities?

The second aspect, describing the *cause* for attaining enlightenment, is divided into two aspects:

— the absence of concepts;
— the presence of discriminating wisdom.

Realizing the empty essence of all phenomena, one does not conceptualize or fixate on anything as being such and such. In the context of the enlightened essence, this is called the *absence of concepts*. Without this quality, one will continue to form ideas about phenomena, thinking 'nice,' 'not nice,' 'neutral,' and so on. Based on these concepts, feelings of attraction, aversion, or indifference arise. Based on our feelings, disturbing emotions surface and the suffering of cyclic existence is perpetuated. Therefore, when concepts — the primary cause of samsaric existence — are cleared away because of insight into the nature of reality, the practitioner can progress along the path to enlightenment. Hence, nonconceptualization is the major cause for attainment of enlightenment.

The secondary cause, discriminating wisdom, coexists with an absence of concepts. This is the wisdom of clear discernment whereby all things are vividly perceived. It is still nonconceptual, but nonconceptual doesn't suggest an utterly blank state, like sleep or oblivion. We shouldn't think an absence of concepts means one is like an idiot who doesn't know right from wrong and just sits in a thoughtless state with a gaping mouth and vacant eyes.

3 — Fruition

This third point describes the fruition of enlightenment, the complete purification of the two obscurations of disturbing emotions and dualistic knowledge.

When the disturbing emotion of attachment vanishes, the enlightened essence is like a lake of pure water strewn with lotus flowers. When the emotion of aggression is purified, it is like the moon which is no longer eclipsed but round and full. When the emotion of stupidity is cleared away, it is like the sun freed from cloud-cover.

When the clouds evaporate, the sun is revealed shining with all its strength. Likewise, once these three disturbing emotions are purified, the perfect qualities are naturally present.

4 — Function

The fourth point is called the function of enlightenment. Complete enlightenment functions as the spontaneous accomplishment of benefit for oneself and others. Achieving the perfect abandonment benefits oneself; accomplishing the perfect realization benefits others.

5 — Endowments

Because enlightenment is free from birth, old age, sickness, and death, it is endowed with the four qualities of permanence, everlastingness, peace, and changelessness.

6 — Manifestation

How does enlightenment manifest? It manifests buddha activity through the three kayas: *dharmakaya, sambhogakaya,* and *nirmanakaya.* Because the two perfections are achieved, one automatically attains the dharmakaya which benefits oneself. Having attained the absolute dharmakaya for the benefit of oneself, one then manifests the two relative forms, sambhogakaya and nirmanakaya, for the benefit of others. These two 'bodies' appear to those who are to be tamed in accordance with their degree of obscuration. Hence, the Buddha appears in the sambhogakaya form to the bodhisattvas dwelling on the ten bhumis.

What is sambhogakaya? The Tibetan word is *longchö dzogpey ku. Longchö* means 'enjoyments,' or 'an abundance of wealth.' This is the literal sense. *Dzogpa* means 'complete' or 'nothing lacking.' Therefore, complete enjoyment. Altogether, sambhogakaya means the body of perfect enjoyments.

How does a perfect enjoyment body relate to enlightenment? We must understand the Buddha's aspiration for sentient beings. He plans to first guide all sentient beings out of the confusion and suffering of samsara and establish them on the pure bodhisattva level. Next, the perfectly enlightened Buddha intends to guide all the bodhisattvas dwelling on the bodhisattva bhumis to complete enlightenment. The latter part of this guidance, which directs the bodhisattvas towards complete buddhahood, is enacted by the sambhogakaya forms. Hence, the enjoyments are actually the fulfillments of the intention to attain enlightenment. 'Perfect' means that those intentions are completely fulfilled.

Normally, *kaya* means 'body' or 'embodiment.' In the case of the two form kayas, 'body' means the embodiment of being able to fulfill one's intentions. In accordance with this, there is the nirmanakaya, the body of magical emanation or manifestation. If the Buddha only emanated sambhogakaya forms, ordinary impure beings would be unable to progress and buddha activity would, therefore, be limited. So, the nirmanakaya is then emanated from the realm of sambhogakaya. Emanations manifest in various ways, either as a *supreme nirmanakaya,* like Buddha Shakyamuni, as a *created nirmanakaya,* as an *incarnate nirmanakaya,* or as a *variegated nirmanakaya,* in accordance with the needs and inclinations of different sentient beings.

In short, enlightenment is a threefold manifestation called the three kayas — the dharmakaya which manifests first as the sambhogakaya and then as the nirmanakaya.

7 — Permanence

Throughout one's existence as an ordinary sentient being until the attainment of complete enlightenment, the buddha-nature itself is utterly unchanging. Therefore, the dharmakaya is said to be essentially permanent. The sambhogakaya has the permanence of continuity in that it continually manifests. It is not essentially permanent, like the dharmakaya, but it is constant in that the sambhogakaya forms turn the Wheel of Dharma without interruption. The sambhogakaya buddha is not born to later pass away, and because of this unceasing existence the sambhogakaya has the permanence of continuity.

The nirmanakaya does not possess essential or continuous permanence, but it has the 'permanence of being uninterrupted.' There is no interruption in the activity of benefitting beings; however, no continuity is maintained as to any particular realm. When a manifestation of the nirmanakaya finishes benefitting sentient beings in a particular realm, it reappears in another time and place to benefit beings.

8 — Inconceivability

Why is the state of buddhahood, with its three kayas, inconceivable? An ordinary person cannot possibly comprehend complete enlightenment because the dharmakaya is actualized from the standpoint of the realization of the absolute nature of things which is beyond the reach of ordinary thought. Therefore, enlightenment is inconceivable.

These eight points explain the fifth vajra topic — enlightenment.

Questions and Answers

STUDENT: Why isn't the obscuration of dualistic knowledge the cause of samsara?

RINPOCHE: Merely conceptualizing subject and object is not the cause for samsara. The emotions which result from conceptualization, such as liking, disliking, and indifference cause samsara. They are based on the obscuration of dualistic knowledge, but we sometimes have the obscuration of dualistic knowledge without the obscuration of disturbing emotions. At that time, the obscuration of dualistic knowledge itself does not cause samsara.

STUDENT: Could you explain the 'variegated nirmanakaya?'

RINPOCHE: 'Variegated nirmanakaya' might not be the perfect translation; it means that the manifestations of nirmanakaya don't necessarily have to be human. For example, a lion, a rabbit, or a mountain deer can be nirmanakayas that either directly or indirectly benefit sentient beings. A created nirmanakaya is, for example, a human being who has not had to take birth, but appears miraculously for a certain length of time.

For instance, one of the Buddha's disciples was named Rabga. He was a king who loved to play the sitar. Rabga was quite accomplished and would play for hours. His companions were also disciples of the Buddha. Though the king had devotion and interest in the Dharma, when the others would go for teachings he preferred to stay at home and play his sitar. For a long time, he did not go for teachings, but eventually the time arrived for the Buddha to convert him.

The Buddha emanated a created nirmanakaya who was a highly skilled musician. The nirmanakaya went to the palace and entered the courtyard where he sat down and started to play his sitar. When the king heard the beautiful music, he thought, "Wow! Here's a really fine musician," and he called out to the nirmanakaya, saying, "Who are you?" The musician answered, "I heard you are a great sitar player so I have come here to compete with you. Would you like to have a contest?" The king agreed and so they went into the king's private chambers and started to play. The Buddha's emanation was winning, which surprised the king because he thought of himself as the best sitar player in the whole world, so they agreed to make the contest even more difficult. They started to cut the sitar's strings so that, with each rendition, their sitars had one less string. Again, the nirmanakaya seemed to be winning. They continued cutting stings until there were no strings left, but each time the nirmanakaya won. Having enlightened abilities, the emanation of Lord Buddha continued to play quite nicely even though his sitar was stringless. [Laughter] The king was, of course, unable to make any music at all on his stringless instrument. In that moment, his pride and self-esteem completely collapsed and he went to receive teachings from the Buddha. That was an example of created nirmanakaya.

STUDENT: Would a nirmanakaya ever manifest as the teacher of a non-Buddhist religion? Must they be Buddhist teachers?

RINPOCHE: It is entirely possible that a nirmanakaya can manifest as any kind of being, such as a lion, rabbit, or as a follower or teacher of another religion. It all depends on whether the nirmanakaya can benefit beings and guide them on the correct path through a particular form. It is possible that these beings may be emanations of the Buddha, but if, through a certain religion, they guide beings on the wrong path, it is certainly not an emanation.

STUDENT: How is the absence of a self-entity realized through practice? Is it easier to recognize the nonexistence of a self-entity in external objects than it is to realize the nonexistence of one's own ego? If one aspect is understood, does understanding of the other naturally follow soon after?

RINPOCHE: It depends on the practice. Following the Hinayana path to attain arhathood, one merely realizes the nonexistence of individual self, of ego. Practicing the bodhisattva path, one recognizes the nonexistence of the self of entities, or external objects. If one practices the Vajrayana teachings of Mahamudra or Dzogchen, one begins by determining what the nature of things truly is. There is an outer as well as an inner nature of external objects and of the mind within, but through practicing Mahamudra or Dzogchen one resolves right away the nature of mind. One thereby understands the nonexistence of both an individual self and a self of things simultaneously.

STUDENT: Please clarify what 'confusion' actually refers to.

RINPOCHE: At present, due to the overwhelming power of ignorance, we are mistaken about the nature of things. With confusion in our mind, we cannot clearly examine how things truly are. For example, while sleeping we may dream that we are in the jungle with a tiger chasing us. The tiger approaches and is about to eat us. We are terrified and want to run away. There isn't much we can do in the dream state because we are unable to block our experience, but if we could just investigate the situation at that time, we would discover that there is really no jungle and no tiger. In fact, none of what seems to be occurring is true, but we are too overwhelmed by our perceptions to stop and closely examine the real situation. Yet, if a clairvoyant person were present who could see that we were dreaming about being lost in a jungle and pursued by a wild animal, that person could shake us and say, "Hey, wake up! Don't be afraid. It's just a dream." At that point, we would wake up and the confusing dream images would disappear. However, left on our own, we are too busy worrying about how to escape our ferocious 'dream tiger' to stop and realize how things really are. In the same way, sentient beings need to depend on the fully enlightened Buddha to convey to us our true condition.

STUDENT: What is meant by 'space' or 'dharmadhatu'?

RINPOCHE: In this context, the word for space is ying. It is the same word used for dhatu in dharmadhatu, the realm or 'space' of things. The word space is used because the dharmadhatu is like the body or realm of empty space where different things, like clouds, birds, and airplanes can fly around without obstruction. This is because the nature of space is empty and nonexistent. Due to this quality of openness, things can occur. Likewise, dharmadhatu is the essence of things — empty and inconcrete — where all phenomena such as trees, houses, mountains, oneself, other beings, emotions, wisdom, and all experiences can occur openly.

Changkya Rölpey Dorje, a lineage guru, sang a song about being a small boy sitting on his mother's lap. Sitting with his back to his mother, he was looking all around. Suddenly, unable to see his mother anywhere, he became very distressed and thought, "Where's my mother! Where's my mother!" [Laughter] Finally, one of his older brothers came along and he asked him, "Where's my mother?" His brother replied, "She's right there behind you." He turned around and found his mother, again. At that moment, he could relax again. [Laughter]

Likewise, dharmadhatu, the space of things, is like our mother. We are always within dharmadhatu, but because we are obscured we think we have to find dharmadhatu somewhere else. So, we look around, thinking, "Where is dharmadhatu? Where is dharmadhatu?" Eventually, through the teachings, we will investigate the nature of things and understand that dharmadhatu is right here.

Student: What is 'luminosity?'

Rinpoche: When we say luminosity, in Tibetan salwa, it does not refer to light or the luminous quality of an electric bulb or the sun. It has little to do with that. Luminosity refers to the intelligent capacity of wakefulness — knowledge and wisdom, or *prajna* and *jnana* — the ability to 'know'. The Second Turning of the Wheel of Dharma emphasizes the emptiness of things, the absence of a self. "There is no I, no nose, no tongue, and so forth." Words such as 'non-existence' and 'space-like' are mentioned a lot. If we understand emptiness as blank, void space without any qualities, then we've missed the mark. Dharmadhatu is not like that. In dharmadhatu, there is constant manifestation of relative appearances that arise due to the law of causation or dependent connection. It's certainly not just a blank or stupid space. It has the luminous quality which expresses itself as intelligent wakefulness. If, when practicing, you look into your mind you will find out what we mean by emptiness and luminosity. Then conviction that the mind is both empty and luminous will grow.

STUDENT: What is the difference between *rangdang* and *rangtsal?*

RINPOCHE: I'm not sure I understand the question. In Tibetan, there are three terms: *shi, dang,* and *tsal. Shi* means the essence is empty, *dang* means whatever manifests is unobstructed, and the third quality, *tsal,* means manifold things can manifest.

STUDENT: Is there a link between the Buddha of Boundless Light and luminosity?

RINPOCHE: Although the root word 'light' is found both in Amitabha and luminosity, there is quite a difference. When we talk about Amitabha, the Buddha of Boundless light, we are not talking about his mind, but about his physical qualities. From each pore in his body, boundless rays of light are emanated and illuminate the universe. In this respect, there's some resemblance to the sun or an electric bulb, but luminosity is not like that. It has nothing to do with light rays. It is the capacity to 'know': intelligence, wakefulness, cognizance.

STUDENT: What is the difference between *dharmadhatu* and *dharmakaya?*

RINPOCHE: Dharmadhatu is what we just explained — the emptiness of things, space. The general meaning of dharmakaya is that, at the time of attaining complete enlightenment, the physical body of an enlightened being is transformed into the body of enlightened qualities, or the dharmakaya, but at that time the body is not concrete or something we can hold with our hands. It is inseparable from the nature of things. The word 'body' in this context is merely a way of referring to this event. The word 'dharma' has many different connotations, but in this context it implies the unmistaken nature of things.

STUDENT: Why can't sentient beings perceive the nature of things?

RINPOCHE: It's like Rölpey Dorje's song. We have been sitting on our mothers lap for a very long time and although the buddhas have given us the teachings, for some reason we haven't yet turned around and found our mother.

STUDENT: Why, what is the reason?

RINPOCHE: Because we haven't looked. [Laughter] We haven't been interested.

STUDENT: Why haven't we been interested?

RINPOCHE: We've been too busy looking at other things. We've had no time to recognize our mother. [Laughter] There are different kinds of children. Some kids like to play around a lot and do all different kinds of things. They make their mothers anxious. But there are other kinds of children who really cherish their mother and like to be close to her. We probably belong to the kind of kids who like to play around a lot. [Laughter] If we don't watch out, playing around so much, in the future we will continue to lose our mother.

STUDENT: What does the word 'dharma' in dharmakaya refer to?

RINPOCHE: The 'dharma' refer to the enlightened qualities that are permanent, everlasting, and changeless. These qualities manifest as the three different kayas. You can understand it that way.

STUDENT: How can wisdom be non-conceptual?

RINPOCHE: Wisdom is realized through the nonconceptual state which, by the way, is not a blank, oblivious state. The nonconceptual state is often likened to the surface of a calm and still lake where the stars and heavenly bodies are reflected clearly and distinctly because the lake has no concept of itself to interfere with the reflection. Therefore, the reflections appear as they naturally are. The lake does not think, "This is Venus, this Mars, this Saturn..." and so on, but still the reflections of all the stars and planets are present very vividly and distinctly.

STUDENT: What is a nirmanakaya?

RINPOCHE: The word nirmanakaya, in Tibetan, *tulku,* means the body which is emanated, or manifested. Why is the nirmanakaya emanated or manifested? For the sole purpose of benefiting sentient beings; it is not emanated to tease people, or harm anybody, or to make money.

STUDENT: If there is no self, no ego, no personality, and no identifying characteristics, what is it that distinguishes one buddha from another?

RINPOCHE: A buddha still has his own mind, but there's no clinging to a false self or ego. For example, in the guru yoga practice of Milarepa, when we pray to Milarepa we should understand that Milarepa's mind is inseparable from the dharmadhatu and that his mind is endowed with perfectly enlightened qualities. Although we have not yet realized the enlightened qualities, our mind co-exists in the same dharmadhatu; therefore, we can receive the blessings of Milarepa's enlightened qualities by making supplication. Receiving the blessings is called *mingling one's mind with the mind of the guru,* but that doesn't mean that we have *become* Milarepa.

STUDENT: It seems that royalty is emphasized in Buddhism.

RINPOCHE: You're right. There are lots of stories about kings as well as stories about ordinary people. But there is a reason why there are more stories about kings. Buddhas have appeared in the past, such as Dipamkara, Kashyapa, and Buddha Shakyamuni. Lord Maitreya will appear in the future as the fifth buddha of this age. Before they appear, buddhas always find out who is considered the highest ranking class among human beings.

For example, because the priest caste was deemed the highest level of beings in the days of Buddha Dipamkara, he appeared as the son of a priest and in that way he was highly respected and it was easier for people to believe in him. As a priest, he naturally had followers. However, at the time of Buddha Shakyamuni, the highest level of beings belonged to the royal caste. Therefore, he appeared as the son of a king because that appealed to people's minds and enabled him to reach and guide a large number of people. Likewise, most of his stories were about kings and nobility because people enjoyed hearing about this class of beings, and they would readily take the parables to heart. However, the coming buddha may take birth among the most democratic group of beings, or perhaps among a socialist group. It is said Buddha Maitreya will manifest as a more ordinary person. How buddhas behave and how they display themselves generally depends upon the times and the kind of people living in those ages. In the past, some people were impressed by means of the Buddha's words, some by means of his behavior, and others by means of his miraculous powers, but these days people are quite different. People are more so-phisticated so a miracle is not considered very impressive. We usually think it some kind of magic trick. It doesn't arouse genuine faith. This is just my own private idea, but if you examine it a little further you may understand something more.

STUDENT: Since the world is full of buddhas and bodhisattvas who are working for the sake of sentient beings, do you think it would be pos-sible to convince a few of them to take jobs in places like the Penta-gon where one wrong move could mean the end of this planet?

RINPOCHE: It's been quite a few years since the nuclear bomb was in-vented, right? And it hasn't been used much. That might be due to a few bodhisattvas in high places. [Laughter]

Qualities

Dharmakaya, the perfect benefit for oneself, and sambhogakaya and nirmanakaya, the perfect benefit for others, are the very foundation for enlightened qualities to arise. Together, sambhogakaya and nirmanakaya are called *rupakaya* or the 'body of form.' Essentially, this means that the benefit for oneself, the dharmakaya, is determined by ultimate truth while the perfect benefit for others, the form kaya, is determined by relative truth.

Generally speaking, the dharmakaya and the rupakaya are endowed with 32 qualities each, or 64 altogether.

The Qualities of Freedom

The dharmakaya is endowed with what are called the qualities of freedom. These qualities are not newly acquired when one attains enlightenment. They are intrinsic to the enlightened essence itself, but when the enlightened essence is obscured by the two obscurations, these qualities are unable to manifest. Nevertheless, when the enlightened essence is freed from the obscurations, the qualities immediately appear.

The Qualities of Maturation

The rupakaya is endowed with what are called the qualities of maturation, or complete ripening. When fruit is not yet ripe, it doesn't taste very good and the shape is not quite right, but with the passage of time it continues to ripen until it eventually obtains a perfect color, shape, and flavor. Likewise, the qualities of the rupakaya — meaning the sambhogakaya and nirmanakaya — are attributes which have reached maturation.

The qualities of freedom are achieved through the direct perception of the truth of reality, dharmata, or, as mentioned previously, through perfecting the qualities of abandonment and realization. Whereas, the qualities of maturation result from the accumulation of merit achieved through engaging in the six paramitas and other virtuous practices.

The thirty-two qualities of freedom include the ten powers of perfect knowledge, the fourfold fearlessness, and the eighteen unique qualities.

The Ten Powers of Perfect Knowledge

Knowing fact from fiction;
Knowing how actions will ripen;
Knowing the faculties of sentient beings;
Knowing their dispositions;
Knowing the inclinations of sentient beings;
Knowing where the various paths lead;
Knowing the concentrations;
Recollecting former states;
Superknowledge of the divine eye;
Knowing the extinction of defilements.

The ten powers are often compared to a vajra because they vanquish all hesitation, doubts, uncertainties, ignorance, and perverted views.

The first of the ten powers is called the power of knowing fact from fiction. Facts are reasonable and true, fiction is both unreasonable and untrue. All errors arise from our inability to discern what is fact and what is fiction. Yet, when complete enlightenment is achieved, one gains a thorough understanding of truth and untruth.

The second power is called the power of knowing how actions will ripen. The moment an action occurs, an enlightened being possesses a direct knowledge of how that action will ripen in the future — for example, he knows that a particular misdeed will result in a particular kind of suffering later on, and that a certain virtuous action will eventually create a certain kind of happiness.

The third power is called the power of knowing the faculties of sentient beings. This refers to a perfect knowledge of the different capacities of sentient beings. There are subtle differences in the faculties of beings. Some people have a lot of faith, but very little diligence and not much intelligence; some are very intelligent, but lack faith and diligence; some are extraordinarily diligent, but haven't much faith and intelligence. Some beings have superior faculties, meaning these people possess more faith, intelligence, compassion, diligence, and so on. Therefore, a fully realized buddha can instruct these beings, according to their capacity, in the more extensive and profound methods and they will be able to understand and practice these teachings. However, there are also beings with lesser faculties. Because they possess little faith, diligence, intelligence, and compassion, it would be pointless for the tathagatas to teach them the vast and profound methods. Since a fully enlightened buddha has the power of knowing the capacities of beings, he will always teach methods that are suitable. Due to the many different kinds of faculties of sentient beings, the buddhas teach accordingly, mainly by means of turning the Wheel of the Dharma. The teachings of the definitive meaning and the expedient meaning are taught to beings of different capacities; nevertheless, both teachings are very profound, significant, and beneficial.

The fourth power is the power of knowing the dispositions — in this context 'dispositions' also refers to the particular scope of mind of a sentient being. Some people like very vast and profound teachings, while others prefer more simple instructions. Therefore, a buddha will give teachings that range from the very extensive to the very simple.

Simply to know the various faculties and dispositions of sentient beings is not sufficient to truly benefit them. An enlightened being must also know their inclinations and interests. Therefore, the fifth power is called the power of knowing the inclinations of sentient beings. Some people think it is more important to practice, rather than spend time studying scriptures or philosophical texts. Others believe it is utterly essential to study texts and develop intellectual understanding, rather than practice. Some people think they must attain something for themselves and that other beings are not very important. There are beings of many different kinds of inclination. Without insight into the various inclinations of beings, a buddha might give a particular teaching to a person whose interests lie elsewhere and the teaching would be of no benefit. Therefore, recognizing the interests of different beings, a fully enlightened buddha teaches accordingly.

The sixth power is called the power of knowing where the various paths lead. Generally speaking, there are Hinayana, Mahayana, and Vajrayana paths. Within Vajrayana, there is the path of *Kriya, Charya,* and *Yoga Tantra* as well as *Anuttara.* Anuttara Tantra is subdivided into Mother Tantra, Father Tantra, and Nondual Tantra. In this way, there are nine *yanas,* or vehicles. A fully enlightened buddha knows where all these different kinds of practices lead, how they should be taught, and so forth. By giving Dharma teachings, a buddha shows sentient beings the path which leads to liberation.

We should also know where different paths lead. If we only know one path, for example, from here to Kathmandu, we can reach our destination traveling this one path. However, should we stray down another path, we may find ourselves in trouble. To use a very gross example, we could say that, in this respect, a buddha must be like a taxi driver — he must know all the different paths in his neighborhood. If a taxi driver knew only one path, he would have to tell his passengers, "I can take you to such and such place, but if you want to go anywhere else, I can't help you." A professional driver must know all the roads because some people like to go down narrow lanes and others prefer smooth, wide avenues.

The seventh power is called the power of knowing the concentrations. These are usually called *dhyana* and *samadhi.* For each of these meditative states, there are various levels and classifications. For example, some meditative states may be mixed with concepts, but possess discernment. Other meditative states may be free of concepts, but lack discernment. Both conceptualization and discernment are absent in some meditative states. Since a fully enlightened being has a complete understanding of the different levels of meditation and concentration, he is able to teach a perfect path to liberation.

The eighth power concerns the past and is called the power of recollecting former states. Again, knowing the dispositions, various inclinations, and faculties of sentient beings as well as where different paths lead is still not sufficient to truly benefit beings. A fully enlightened buddha must know the past and the future. He should possess a complete knowledge of past events regarding the former lives and activities of sentient beings, where and when they were born, what they did in each past life, and so on.

The ninth power concerns the future and is called the super-knowledge of the divine eye. With this knowledge, a buddha can see when and where a particular sentient being will die, when and where he will subsequently take rebirth, and, having taken rebirth, the kinds of joys and sorrows he will undergo.

The tenth power is called the power of knowing the extinction of defilements. 'Defilement' refers to the two obscurations — the obscuration of disturbing emotions and the obscuration of dualistic knowledge. Complete enlightenment is totally free because all defilements have been exhausted. Before attaining enlightenment, even the Buddha was burdened by these two obscurations, but after having followed the path he freed himself from them. Because he has realized the state free from defilements, he therefore knows the various methods that produce buddhahood.

The Four Types of Fearlessness

In this context, 'fearlessness' is symbolized by the strong and powerful lion who need fear no other animal. With his stability of mind, he is never afraid that a tiger or an elephant might attack him. The lion possesses absolute self-confidence and fearlessness. Likewise, a fully enlightened buddha has no fear of being attacked.

The first of the four types of fearlessness is called fearlessness in proclaiming the mastery of the perfect abandonment. Because a buddha has totally cast away all that should be abandoned, he is not afraid to proclaim this. If someone were to announce that they had totally mastered the perfect abandonment, though he might not be challenged, if that were untrue the person would lack total self-confidence when making such a proclamation. But in the case of a buddha, no one can challenge his word and say, "That's not true. You still must purify such and such defilement."

The second fearlessness is called fearlessness in proclaiming the mastery of perfect realization. Here, in the same way, because a buddha has perfect realization in all respects, no one can object and say, "There is still a path you haven't realized. Though you have realized quite a lot, but there is still more to learn." The perfectly enlightened being has realized 100% of what must be realized.

The first two kinds of fearlessness refer to the enlightened being, himself. The next two kinds refer to others.

The third fearlessness is called fearlessness in showing the path. An enlightened being never has any doubt as to when and how to show the path to sentient beings. He never has doubts about his ability to guide beings.

The fourth fearlessness is called fearlessness in revealing hindrances on the path. A buddha never hesitates, wondering, "Will the teaching I am giving become a hindrance to this person's practice or create confusion is his mind?" A buddha never fears obstacles on the path.

The Eighteen Unique Qualities

Here, 'unique' describes qualities which are unshared or exclusive to the fully enlightened state and are not possessed by bodhisattvas or pratyekabuddhas. They are like space. Space can be found in combination with either earth, water, fire, or wind. However, none of these elements — earth, fire, water, wind — possess the open, expansive quality of the space element. Likewise, since the qualities of complete enlightenment are not shared by even the bodhisattvas, they are called unique qualities.

The eighteen unique qualities can be grouped into sets of four. The first set of the eighteen qualities concerns the behavior of the body, speech, and mind of an enlightened being. The second set concerns realization, the perfect understanding of wisdom knowledge. The third set concerns activity. The fourth set concerns the wisdoms. As a whole, they refer to enlightened behavior, realization, activity, and wisdom.

Ordinary people like ourselves often make mistakes in our physical activities. Even an arhat may possibly take a mistaken step, such as stepping on a snake. However, the physical behavior of a buddha is never mistaken or confused. It is utterly impossible for a fully enlightened buddha to make even a single error in his bodily actions. In addition, a buddha's physical behavior is never pointless and is always beneficial. We ordinary beings move our head from side to side in order to see something, but there is no real point to such activity and we accrue no benefit from it whatsoever. Yet, when a buddha turns his head in a particular direction, that simple act serves a definite purpose and a certain benefit also results.

Secondly, the Buddha's speech is free of idle talk or meaningless utterances. Sometimes we say things which are totally pointless, without any benefit whatsoever. In fact, our careless chatter can directly harm others because we can say things which will create attachment, aggression, or delusion in the minds of others. But when the Buddha utters a word, it is always for a definite reason and immense benefit is always derived from it.

A fully enlightened buddha's presence of mind is never impaired. We sometimes say, "I forget!" but it is impossible for a fully enlightened buddha to say, "I forgot to benefit sentient beings." His timing and the method used to benefit others is impeccable, with unfailing presence of mind.

The fourth quality is that a buddha's mind is always completely composed, always resting in equanimity or evenness. For example, ordinary people like ourselves are continuously distracted by conceptual thoughts. There's never even a moment of resting in evenness or composure. The bodhisattva experiences periods of meditation and periods of post-meditation, but during periods of meditation, or composure, a bodhisattva is unable to benefit beings, and, when benefiting beings, he is unable to rest in composure. But the fully enlightened being has totally mingled meditation and post-meditation so regardless of whether he is giving a Dharma talk or walking on the street, his mind is totally resting in the composure of the nature of reality, dharmata. Never, for even an instance, is he without presence of mind.

The fifth quality states that a buddha is beyond holding many ideas. Here, 'ideas' means different considerations. For example, we are usually caught up in an on-going stream of mental activity deliberating what possible actions to take in any given situation, but a buddha is beyond that. Because he possesses the supreme understanding of what any situation calls for, his actions are always exactly appropriate and he need never ponder or deliberate about what to do.

The sixth quality refers to a buddha's freedom from indifference or carelessness. Sometimes, we spend time with a friend talking about many different things. Although we originally intended to say something beneficial and guide that person towards the Dharma, instead the time is consumed discussing ordinary worldly affairs so that afterwards we think, "I should have told him about such and such, but I forgot. I didn't think of it." Or it sometimes happens that we were supposed to visit a person because we could benefit them in some way, but, for some reason we didn't go. Perhaps we were delayed or we just became indifferent. However, a buddha never falls under the power of carelessness or indifference. His actions are never delayed, but are always precise and dependable like the sea. High and low tide always occur at definite, regular times that are never delayed.

These six qualities describe a buddha's behavior. His realization also possesses six qualities. The first three refer to intention, exertion, and presence of mind, or intelligence. The next three refer to the unimpeded cognition of past, present, and future. These six qualities comprise the qualities of realization.

Following this, there are three qualities of activity. The first of these qualities describes how a buddha's actions are always preceded by wisdom and always followed by clear cognizance. For example, when ordinary beings pick something up from a table, we don't give it much thought or consideration. We just take the object. Because many of our actions are done while in this careless frame of mind, we often make mistakes that create problems in the future. But a buddha never makes such errors. All his actions are preceded by wisdom which means he has already examined the reason for acting and the benefit which will result so that when he performs the action he knows what the outcome will be. In the same way, his actions are always followed by wisdom in that he knows what he has done, what its purpose was, and what benefit will accrue.

The second quality refers to speech. Again, an enlightened being's speech is both preceded by wisdom and followed by wisdom. We sometime speak and then later regret what we have said. We think, "I shouldn't have said that. Now, all this trouble is arising from that statement."

The third quality refers to mental actions. Whatever occurs in a buddha's mind is cognized and known while it takes place. It is not like our frivolous, uninhibited thought patterns.

Three aspects comprise the quality of wisdom. The first of these is the wisdom that perceives the past exactly as it was; the second is the wisdom that perceives the future exactly as it will be, and the third is the wisdom that perceives the present exactly as it is.

Altogether, these comprise the 32 qualities of freedom. The 32 qualities of freedom are said to be like the moon in the sky and the 32 qualities of maturation are likened to the reflection of the moon on the surface of water. What exists in the sky is exactly what is reflected in the water. The reflection of these qualities manifests as the *32 excellent major marks* of either the sambhogakaya or the nirmana-kaya. They are called the natural form of the qualities of freedom. These 32 major marks are quite easy to understand. We can read the list in the translation.

Questions and Answers

STUDENT: I don't really understand what 'nirvana' means.

RINPOCHE: The Buddhist term *nirvana* has three connotations. According to the Hinayana vehicle, nirvana is the 'state of arhathood,' according to the pratyekabuddhas, it is 'pratyekabuddha arhathood,' and according to the bodhisattva or the Mahayana vehicle, it is 'complete and true enlightenment.'

STUDENT: Can Rinpoche explain how the five paths of the Mahayana vehicle correlate to the five paths of Vajrayana and the *four yogas of Mahamudra*. Are they different?

RINPOCHE: The five paths themselves, whether Mahayana or Vajrayana, possess no great difference at all. In both cases, it is the same principle of gradual progress. Nevertheless, since the practice of Mahamudra is simply resting in naturalness, there are actually no categories such as paths and levels. Still, these systems can be related to each other.

Each of the *four yogas* has three stages which are called lesser, medium, and greater. The first of the four yogas is *One-pointedness*. The lesser and medium stages of the first yoga, One-pointedness, correspond to the path of accumulation, and the higher stage corresponds to the path of joining. *Simplicity,* the second Mahamudra yoga, corresponds to the path of seeing. The path of cultivation is equal to the three stages of *One Taste,* the third yoga, in their entirety as well as the first two stages of *Nonmeditation.* The highest stage of the fourth Mahamudra yoga, Nonmeditation, corresponds to the path of no more training — complete enlightenment itself.

STUDENT: Could Rinpoche please define ignorance in terms of its being one of the five poisons?

RINPOCHE: Ignorance is not exactly one of the five poisons, but is the basis, the ground, for the five poisons to arise. Ignorance means 'not knowing,' not understanding the nature of what is true. Because of not-knowing, it is possible for the five poisons to arise.

STUDENT: Isn't ignorance one of the three fundamental poisons?

RINPOCHE: This is confusion created by the translators because they use the same English word for two different Tibetan words. One term is *marigpa*, ignorance, the other is *timug*, stupidity or dullness.

STUDENT: Doesn't there have to be some kind of dullness or darkness of mind, blank stupidity, to be called *timug*?

RINPOCHE: Among the five poisons, the kind of stupidity referred to is called *timug*. The literal meaning of *ti* is a full stop. *Mug* means 'obscured,' 'dull,' and 'unclear.' Because of this dullness, we are unable to understand the exact nature of things. It is quite similar to *marigpa*, or ignorance, but it is more a kind of stupidity.

STUDENT: Why is there ignorance?

RINPOCHE: Because the enlightened essence is empty in essence and luminous in nature, a natural display appears. Anything at all can manifest. When manifestations occur, we experience them, but without understanding that they are the expression our own nature — everything is self-manifestation. Because of this confusion, we misapprehend our experiences and ignorance takes over.

For example, there is a blank, empty screen in a movie theater. In the back of the room, a very powerful light bulb projects rays of light through a strip of film. Because of these conditions coming together, the luminosity of the projector's lamp and the filmstrip, all kinds of images are projected on the blank screen. When we look around the room, we can see it is just a cinema screen, a projection, and we can easily understand we're just watching a movie, but when we sit absorbed in watching the scenario we completely forget our true surroundings and we mistakenly think real people are running around on the screen and that something is actually taking place. Our basic ignorance is like this kind of mix-up and confusion.

STUDENT: Can you explain the different kinds of disturbing emotions?

RINPOCHE: There are two kinds of disturbing emotion: manifest and latent. 'Manifest aggression' is when we actually experience anger. 'Latent aggression' refers to the readiness to become angry. 'Latent' in Tibetan is *bagchak* which can be likened to a Tibetan ceremonial scarf which is heavily starched and inflexible. A substance has been applied to the cloth to make it stiff, but we can't really see what the substance is.

Right now, I'm not angry. At this moment, I'm relaxed and feel no aggression whatsoever. Nevertheless, if someone were to say something very unpleasant, I would become irritated and angry. Therefore, our *latent* disturbing emotion is the *potential* for anger to arise. Our *manifest* disturbing emotion is the time of anger's actual arising, or manifestation.

STUDENT: Is there a specific sequence when purifying disturbing emotions on the bodhisattva stages?

RINPOCHE: Purification is a process on the path. When we reach the first bhumi, the gross manifest emotions will have already been purified; therefore, the subtle latent emotions will be easy to purify. Though these are actually quite dense, they're easy to purify once one has entered the path and developed the strong concentration of samadhi.

STUDENT: Previously, you mentioned habitual patterns and used the lingering odor of musk as an example. Today, you talked about inherent obscurations. Are habitual patterns and inherent obscurations the same thing?

RINPOCHE: No, they're quite different. The dividing line is between manifest and latent habitual patterns. Tibetans have only a single definition for 'latent' and 'habitual.' The 'imputed' and the 'inherent' both belong to manifest defilements. The imputed is what we learn after growing up; for instance, we believe our religion is right and that other religions are wrong. We are conditioned to hold onto particular ideas as true. Whereas, the inherent refers to what a small child does naturally — certain mental concepts that are already inherent in the child. They both belong to the manifest.

STUDENT: Because they are momentary, the imputed gross obscurations are not actually inherent to the enlightened essence. Could Rinpoche comment more on what they actually are?

RINPOCHE: These obscurations belong to confusion, or bewilderment. According to the Sutra system, the enlightened essence is like a jewel covered with mud or old cloth. According to Vajrayana, when receiving the pointing-out instruction one recognizes one's own essence. At that instant, the obscurations are momentarily absent. However, when one forgets one's essence and again turns one's attention towards external objects, one becomes distracted and the obscurations are back again.

STUDENT: Are the obscurations themselves a part of the enlightened essence, but perceived incorrectly?

RINPOCHE: Yes, you can say that. But it is because of not perceiving the enlightened essence, itself, correctly that one is confused and obscurations arise.

STUDENT: Do all beings have obscurations or is it dependent upon one's karma?

RINPOCHE: All sentient beings have these obscurations. They are not dependent upon karma at all. They are called inherent because they are intrinsic to being a sentient being and arise automatically by themselves. Whereas karma is something that is abandoned before the subtle obscurations are abandoned. Karma is already abandoned prior to entering the path of seeing. Therefore, subtle obscurations could not be dependent upon karma. Take, for example, an ear of corn. It has layers on the outside which you can peel off until you reach the ear of corn on the inside, yet the corn inside has always been there.

STUDENT: Obscurations are not abandoned and cleared away until the path of seeing? What are we doing before that? If the gross disturbing emotions are not purified until the path of seeing, what are beginners doing?

TRANSLATOR: The nine levels of purifying obscurations concern the inherent obscurations.

RINPOCHE: When we refer to the *five paths,* the first and second are called the path of accumulation and the path of joining. They are not included in the ten bhumis.

The first bhumi starts with the third path, the path of seeing. The second bhumi starts with the fourth path, the path of cultivation. The second to the ninth bhumis are all included within the path of cultivation. At the fifth path, there are no more bhumis. They are finished. That is called the path of no more training, complete and perfect enlightenment. All ten bhumis are included within the third and the fourth path, the path of seeing and the path of cultivation.

STUDENT: Could one use clouds in the sky to illustrate the lack of inherent existence of obscurations?

RINPOCHE: It is true that the obscurations are momentary, like a cloud in the sky. Unless some other circumstance occurs, like a strong wind, the cloud will remain. Likewise, the obscurations, although momentary, will not disappear unless some remedy is applied. The primary cause that triggers rebirth in samsara is the inherent obscurations. But they are not enough. Just having inherent obscurations doesn't mean that one immediately takes rebirth in a certain manner. Rebirth is due to karma. Karma determines where and how one is born, in which realm, whether rich or poor, clever or stupid and so forth. However, the primary basis for continuing in samsara is the subtle inherent obscurations.

STUDENT: Would Rinpoche please give us a few examples of subtle obscurations.

RINPOCHE: The example given before was musk in a bottle. After musk is removed from a bottle and the bottle is washed with soap and water, some musky odor still lingers. Likewise, when dwelling on the high bodhisattva bhumis, although the gross disturbing emotions and negative emotions are cast away, there is still some subtle trace of habitual pattern for these emotions to reappear. In our present state, they are not evident or obvious at all; they are very subtle and latent.

When proceeding through the bodhisattva bhumis, one starts by purifying the gross obscurations which gradually thin out and vanish. One begins with a mild remedy and then slowly applies a stronger and stronger remedy. This corresponds to the obscurations arising less and less often. It is very easy to wash and scrub a large piece of material, but washing a tiny swatch of cloth is more difficult and takes more time and concentration. Likewise, the most subtle obscurations require a strong practice, a tremendously powerful remedy, to purify them. The final obscuration of dualistic knowledge is purified by the strongest antidote which is called the *vajra-like samadhi*. This state of samadhi clears away the last remainders of the most subtle innate obscuration.

Buddha Activity

After attaining enlightenment, one's enlightened qualities function as buddha activity — the seventh vajra topic.

Buddha activity has two aspects:

— spontaneously present activity;
— unceasing activity.

Spontaneously Present Activity

What does spontaneously present activity mean? It means 'effortless' activity. When a political system tries to propagate its philosophy, a great deal of effort and struggle is often required. Either an enormous expenditure is made to finance the cause or a large army is employed to enforce the system. But buddha activity is not like that. The Buddha didn't have to spend a lot of money to finance Buddhism. He didn't need a huge army to enforce his teachings nor did he have to exert much effort at all. Nevertheless, although 2500 years have passed since the Buddha entered Parinirvana, his teachings have spread throughout many countries and cultures. This is a direct result of the spontaneously present activity.

When the Buddha was physically present on this planet, he gave the 84,000 Dharma teachings. In those days, there were 2500 arhats who had attained a high level of realization. Their accomplishment was not due to any effort on the Buddha's part. It was the result of spontaneous buddha activity. When the time was right for the spread of the Hinayana teachings to benefit beings, the spontaneous buddha activity fulfilled this need. Later on, the time was ripe for the Mahayana teachings to become widespread for the sake of benefitting beings. Later still, the Vajrayana teachings proliferated. However, the Buddha didn't think, "Now, we should spread the Hinayana teachings," or "Now, the Mahayana teachings are required," or "Now, we should give Vajrayana teachings." It is never like that. The spontaneous and continuously present buddha activity effectuates these different teachings at different time periods.

When there are Hinayana students to be tamed, the Hinayana teachings flourish naturally. When there are Mahayana students to be tamed, the Mahayana teachings flourish automatically and it is the same with the Vajrayana teachings. The activity arises naturally, effortlessly, and spontaneously. Explained in terms of geography, the Hinayana teachings spread from Bodhgaya towards the southern part of India into Sri Lanka, Burma, Thailand, and so forth. Mahayana teachings were propagated north from India, chiefly into China. From China, the teachings spread to Korea and Japan. The Vajrayana teachings spread from India to her neighbor, Nepal, and then to Tibet. From Tibet, the teachings penetrated Mongolia and so on. This did not occur according to a specific plan. It was a natural, effortless, and spontaneous evolvement. Wherever and whenever sentient beings become suitable vessels for such teachings, the Dharma automatically spreads to fulfill the need.

When the Buddha gave a teaching, he did not have to evaluate the disposition of the sentient beings to be tamed and then determine what methods were needed to instruct them. For the Buddha, the act of choosing the appropriate teaching for the appropriate time, place, and recipients is effortless and spontaneous.

For example, when the Buddha first turned the Wheel of Dharma in Varanasi, teaching the Four Noble Truths to the Five Excellent Beings, he did not have to force people to gather around him and listen. He did not plan the teaching, thinking, "I will teach them the Four Noble Truths." It was not a deliberate act, but both spontaneous and effortless. The Second and Third Turning of the Wheel of Dharma were equally unplanned and effortlessly taught.

Unceasing Activity

Unceasing activity reflects the Buddha's unrelenting, boundless compassion. What is compassion? Compassion is the sincere wish that sentient beings be freed from their misery and attain lasting happiness. Because the buddhas are continuously concerned with the welfare of sentient beings, their activity to fulfill the wishes of beings is inexhaustible. In short, because the Buddha's compassion is ceaseless, enlightened activity is also uninterrupted.

Once there was a Chinese man who died and went to hell. Somehow, this particular hell realm resembled a Chinese restaurant where people were seated at a huge table covered with many different plates of Chinese food. Though the food looked delicious, the people were suffering terribly. Why? Because their chopsticks were six feet long. One could manage to pick the food off one's plate, but it was utterly impossible to turn the chopsticks around and put the morsel into one's mouth.

The newcomer stood for a moment, awestruck at the strange sight, when suddenly someone appeared and told him, "Hey. There's been a mistake. You're not supposed to be here. You're supposed to go to that *other* place." In the next instant, the fellow found himself in heaven and once again was faced by the scene of scores of people seated at a huge banquet table covered with plates of Chinese food. Again, the chopsticks were six-feet long, but no one was suffering. Instead, the people seated at the table were feeding each other. People on the left were being fed across the table by people on the right and vice-versa. It's not a true story, of course, but a good illustration. The Buddha said that suffering arises from selfishness while happiness stems from the wish to benefit others.

The Uttara Tantra cites several examples to elucidate the continuous, unceasing activities of enlightenment. These analogies describe how the Buddha's physical form appears effortlessly to sentient beings, how the Dharma is taught both perpetually and without exertion, and how the enlightened state of the Buddha's mind perpetuates spontaneously and continuously. The examples are only analogies used to represent the truth and are not to be taken literally.

Legend has it that Indra, king of the gods, resides in a place called the Palace of Complete Victory. There, in perfect enjoyment and abundant happiness, he abides with a great entourage of gods and goddesses. It is said that if someone down on earth has a large, absolutely smooth, and highly polished mirror-like lapis stone, Indra and all the activities in his kingdom will appear reflected in stone. If ordinary people could see his heavenly enjoyments and the splendor of

Indra's wealth and possessions and know that they are the reward for virtuous actions, people would be encouraged to practice virtuous actions. That's the analogy.

According to this analogy, Indra has no wish to have his reflection appear in a lapis stone somewhere. It is not a deliberate act on his part, yet it happens automatically. Still, it is not pointless. There is an effect — it encourages people to practice virtue. Likewise, essentially, the Buddha's mind does not engender the deliberate intention to appear at such and such place to teach the Dharma. A buddha's appearance in the world is totally spontaneous and effortless, as are the gradual spread of his teachings.

Another example is that of the great drum that resounds throughout the god realm. Due to their vast merit, the gods possess a huge drum that is located in the center of Indra's palace. Spontaneously, it emits the sound of the *Four Seals of the Dharma:*

> All composite things are impermanent;
> All conditioned states are painful;
> All phenomena are empty and devoid of self-nature;
> Nirvana is peace.

The drum does not conceptualize about the sound it emits. This activity is not deliberately planned, but originates effortlessly. This example symbolizes the Buddha's activity of speech. The Buddha never thinks, "Now I must give the Mahayana teachings to such and such person and give the Hinayana teachings to that other person. A buddha speaks spontaneously. His words are then understood by the different individuals as being either a Hinayana or Mahayana teaching. The effect of the Buddha's spontaneous speech is that it naturally benefits countless beings.

A third example is that of a rain cloud. Sometimes clouds appear in the sky and produce rain. Due to the rainfall, plants, trees, bushes, and flowers start to grow. But the cloud doesn't think, "I should send down some rain so the flowers can grow." The Buddha's mind is like this. He never thinks, "I should feel compassion now because its beneficial for sentient beings." These three examples portray the effortless, spontaneous, and nonconceptual qualities of the Buddha's body, speech, and mind.

What are the Buddha's emanations like? The first example is that of the god, Brahma. Although he remains in the Brahma realm, he can still send out emanations that appear in the lower god realms. Without moving from his abode in Brahma Loka, these emanations carry out his various wishes. Likewise, without moving from the nature of dharmakaya, the Buddha can manifest as the sambhogakaya and the supreme nirmanakaya who work for the benefit of beings.

Just as the sun does not deliberately try to shine, but sends forth its rays naturally, automatically, and without any exertion, all the Buddha's wisdom manifestations are constantly ablaze with the radiant qualities of knowledge, compassion, and abilities.

Like a wishfulfilling gem, the mystery of the Buddha's mind is inconceivable. Here, the mystery signifies that it is impossible for ordinary beings to conceive of the actual state of the Buddha's mind. It is said to be like a wishfulfilling gem because such an object fulfills the wishes of the different beings in countless ways. In the same manner, utilizing either the expedient or the definitive meaning of the Dharma, the Buddha's mind fulfills the wishes of sentient beings through giving teachings which accord with their interests and needs.

Another example is that of an echo. This symbolizes the mystery of the Buddha's speech which resounds both effortlessly and naturally, just as an echo appears effortlessly, without any deliberation.

Space naturally permeates everywhere. Like space, the manifestations of the Buddha emanate naturally and effortlessly, reaching wherever they are needed. This example depicts the inconceivable mystery of the Buddha's body and emanations.

Lastly, Buddha activity is like the earth which accommodates all pure phenomena, such as beautiful flowers, precious gemstones, and treasures that lie deep within the soil and also all impure phenomena, such as debris and waste products. The earth makes no preference about what it supports. Likewise, all-encompassing buddha activity embraces all sentient beings, regardless of whether they are pure bodhisattvas, arhats, pratyekabuddhas, or just ordinary, defiled sentient beings. Buddhas do not think, "These beings are already bodhisattvas so they don't need our compassion." Even bodhisattvas on the tenth bhumi are regarded with compassion by the buddhas. At the same time, the buddhas regard ordinary beings who are completely engrossed in the disturbing emotions of jealousy, pride, anger, and so forth with the same all-encompassing compassion. They never think, "We can't help these beings. There's no need to have compassion for them because there's nothing we can do to reach them." Because compassionate Buddha activity accommodates everything, like the earth, it is very basic.

The first three examples, that of Indra, the drum, and the rain cloud, represent the mystery of the Buddha's body, speech, and mind. They exemplify the effortless, spontaneous quality of buddha activity. The examples of Brahma, the echo, and the wishfulfilling gem illustrate the inconceivable nature of buddha activity.

Questions and Answers

STUDENT: Would Rinpoche say a little more about the Four Yogas of Mahamudra?

RINPOCHE: The *Four Yogas of Mahamudra* are called One-pointedness, Simplicity, One Taste, and Nonmeditation. What is the dividing line between these four yogas? Ordinarily, the four yogas begin with the practices of shamatha and vipashyana and culminate with nonmeditation, the attainment of complete enlightenment.

One-pointedness signifies that the mind is able to abide perfectly on an object of concentration. An ordinary person who has not practiced meditation is many-pointed. His concentration is diffused and scattered in many directions. Training in one-pointedness, the practitioner learns to focus his or her mind in one direction and concentrate on a single point.

Recognizing the mind essence exactly as it is, one discovers that the buddha-nature is utterly free from all complexities. *Simplicity* relates to the realization of this uncomplicated aspect of the enlightened essence.

When a single drop of water dissolves in the sea, it becomes one in nature with the whole ocean. Likewise, although phenomena manifest differently, the nature of mind experiences things as being of a single flavor. Therefore, as one's recognition of mind essence increases, one enters the stage called *one-taste* whereby all one's experiences, all phenomena, are understood to have the same nature or 'taste.'

Nonmeditation, or non-cultivation, indicates that one has actually achieved full realization of the nature of things, the essential state of reality. At that point, there's no need to cultivate anything because the state has already been realized. We must cultivate recognition of the enlightened essence in the lower yogas, but once this state has been actualized, there's no need to do anything extra. One can just leave it as it is. For this reason, complete realization is called non-meditation.

STUDENT: How are ordinary people able to perceive the nirmanakaya forms?

RINPOCHE: If one's habitual patterns are very dense, one will not be able to meet enlightened emanations and receive teachings. So, it is depends on one's own karmic pattern. If enough merit has been accumulated, one will be able to meet such emanations. Moreover, if there were no buddha activity, there would be no emanations and no teachings. Still, whether or not the teachings are practiced and whether or not they have an effect depends solely upon oneself. Otherwise, the buddhas would be no different from a Supreme Godhead who just arbitrarily purifies and liberates everybody.

STUDENT: Why do enlightened beings grow old and die?

RINPOCHE: There are two ways of understanding phenomena: how things appear and how things really are. On the level of how things appear, the buddhas send out emanations who take birth, grow old, become ill, and die. This relative aspect of truth accords with the shared perception of sentient beings, but on the level of how things actually are, none of these things really exist. Enlightened emanations do not appear, let alone take birth, grow old, become ill, and die. Nevertheless, in the experience of sentient beings, it certainly appears as though a buddha is born, lives for a while, gets sick, and finally dies.

STUDENT: To what extent do sentient beings exist? Is it because they are perceived by another confused being?

RINPOCHE: Other sentient beings do not exist due to our conceptions or thoughts. They exist due to their own conceptions and thoughts. Dharmakirti established all apparent phenomena as being mind. He explained that houses, trees, mountains, and so forth, even the hell realms, have no true objective existence. They are all just mental experiences, mental perceptions. However, in another context, there is something called the nature of others, meaning other people's minds. What you experience and what I experience is not the same. You can experience something I don't experience; I can experience something you don't experience. Therefore, we must consider the nature of others.

STUDENT: When a sentient being attains complete enlightenment, how does this event affect the rest of the beings in the universe? Because of the ultimate oneness of everything, generally speaking, does the lot of sentient beings as a whole improve at that time? For example, if a diamond is woven into the fabric of an ordinary piece of cloth, the cloth is suddenly greatly enhanced.

RINPOCHE: No, nothing whatsoever changes for other beings. For instance, Milarepa, Marpa, Tilopa, and Naropa realized appearance and existence as the mandala of all-encompassing purity, but their realization didn't help us much, did it?

STUDENT: We weren't there then, were we?

RINPOCHE: We might not have been in their presence, but we were alive somewhere.

STUDENT: What are the 'four seals of the view'?

RINPOCHE: The *four seals of the view* substantiate that a teaching is truly the words of the Buddha, himself. Just as a king uses his royal insignia as a seal to notarize documents so the public can know a declaration is the king's command, likewise four seals, or statements, identify a teaching issued by the fully enlightened Buddha. If a teaching possesses these four seals, it is an enlightened teaching. If a teaching contradicts these four aspects, then it is not.

The first of these seals is that *all compounded things are impermanent*. All that is created is perishable. Secondly, *all conditioned states are painful*. Here, 'conditioning' pertains to the disturbing emotions — the basic cause of suffering. If a teaching concurs with these two facts, it is in compliance with the words of the Buddha. Thirdly, *nirvana is peace*. This implies the absence of negative emotions, karmas, and so forth. Lastly, *all phenomena are empty*. Whatever appears or can be experienced possesses essentially no concrete self and is therefore empty of a self-entity. These are known as the *four seals of the view*, also called the *four great summaries of Dharma* which certify that a teaching was given by the Buddha.

STUDENT: Can you clarify the example of the echo as an analogy for the Buddha's speech?

RINPOCHE: The example of the echo is not used to indicate the law of cause and effect — like somebody standing in a canyon and shouting "Hello!" and the canyon 'answering' "Hello!" That's not the point.

The idea is that the resounding of an echo doesn't involve any thought process or deliberate action on the part of the echo itself. At a certain point, though audible, we can't say exactly where the echo comes from. In the same way, the essence of the Buddha's speech is empty, but still audible. It's not like real sound that has a specific, traceable source.

STUDENT: How can *rigpa* be equated with compassion?

RINPOCHE: When we say *rigpa* is nonconceptual compassion we mean that, although the essence of the Buddha's compassion is empty, boundless compassion still exists for sentient beings because they are confused and mistaken. If sentient beings were not mistaken, there would be no point in having compassion for them. Hence, because a need exists for the Dharma teachings to be given, they appear in the minds of those who are ready to listen. They do not, however, appear in the nonconceptual mind, or perception, of the Buddha himself.

The Buddha said, "Sentient beings perceive that I teach the Dharma. It appears to them as though someone is teaching, it appears as though something is being said, and it appears as though beings are receiving a method for realizing the nature of things. But actually no such thing is taking place at all. The whole thing is arising as the deluded experience of sentient beings." The Buddha only perceives the knowledge of how things truly are. He does not experience these mistaken perceptions.

STUDENT: But he does see beings. Yet, don't beings appear to him as deities? Wouldn't he perceive a mandala of deities?

RINPOCHE: Let's say a person is asleep and experiencing a nightmare. He is dreaming that a tiger is chasing him through a dark jungle and he's terrified. Yet, sitting beside him is another person who is clairvoyant and can perceive that this sleeping person is in the midst of a nightmare. He knows that what this person is experiencing is not true, that the person is actually lying in bed having a dream. So, he will do something to try and wake the poor fellow up. The buddhas are like the clairvoyant person in our example and sentient beings are like the dreamer. The buddhas perceive that ordinary sentient beings are deluded and under the influence of mistaken experiences. Unable to perceive the nature of things — the all-encompassing purity of deities or whatever you prefer to call it, sentient beings suffer. Therefore, teachings are necessary. The clairvoyant person who perceives someone suffering in the dream state feels the need to wake him up. Of course, essentially there is nothing wrong with sleeping — the person is just lying safely on his bed — but because the dreamer's experience is untrue, it's better that his perception be awakened.

STUDENT: But do they appear as deities?

RINPOCHE: Whether or not the Buddha perceives sentient beings as male and female deities is not important because sentient beings don't perceive themselves that way. If the Buddha perceived sentient beings as already pure, there would be no point in giving Dharma teachings. After all, if someone is sleeping very peacefully and someone else awakens him, the person would probably be furious. But if a person is experiencing a nightmare and another person awakens him, he would probably say, "Thanks a lot!"

Conclusion

Try to keep the Seven Vajra Topics in mind while practicing the Dharma. If we study these seven vajra topics with strong enthusiasm, the merit accrued is said to be even greater than if we were to continuously offer an entire universe filled with gold and ornamented with precious jewels to all the buddhas of the three times and ten directions. In fact, listening to and assimilating the seven vajra topics generates more merit than that accumulated by a bodhisattva who maintains perpetual discipline in body, speech, and mind for many aeons. Furthermore, engendering strong faith and trust in the contents of this text gathers more merit than if one were to practice the four concentrations, the *dhyanas,* for a very long period of time. Finally, the Uttara Tantra, itself, declares that studying these seven vajra topics accumulates even greater merit than engaging in the practice of the paramitas of generosity, discipline, and meditation.

How can just learning a text like this accumulate more merit than practicing the paramitas of generosity, discipline, and meditation? Cultivating generosity yields tremendous merit which will result in the eventual accumulation of personal wealth and possessions. Maintaining discipline brings untold merit which will culminate in the achievement of happiness and a perfect body in one of the higher realms. Finally, as a result of perfecting concentration in meditation, one's mind will abide peacefully in shamatha and all one's disturbing emotions will be temporarily suppressed. What could be more important than developing these three superb qualities?

The main hindrances to achieving liberation from samsara and complete enlightenment are the *two obscurations:* the obscuration of disturbing emotions and the obscuration of dualistic knowledge. Therefore, it is absolutely essential that we purify and dispel these veils. Ultimately, the only remedy that can clear them away is *prajna* — the special kind of knowledge which arises from meditation practice. Since no other method can eliminate these obscurations, the development of prajna is an utterly crucial aspect of the path to buddhahood. But how is prajna generated?

There are three kinds of knowledge: the knowledge ensuing from learning, the knowledge ensuing from reflection, and the knowledge ensuing from meditation. Through the knowledge which arises from meditation, we can slowly purify the obscuration of disturbing emotions, the obscuration of dualistic knowledge, and the very subtle obscuration of habitual patterns. Apart from the ultimate outcome of complete enlightenment, genuine bodhichitta will take birth in our being as an immediate benefit. Cultivating bodhichitta strengthens our intention to achieve enlightenment so that diligence, concentration, and knowledge will naturally evolve. With the continual aspiration of bodhichitta, a bodhisattva will not fall victim to further defilements, and the final fruition will be quickly attained.

But how can we develop such extraordinary knowledge? Primarily, enlightenment is attained through perfecting the two qualities of *abandonment and realization.* Prajna arises from studying and reflecting upon the words of Lord Buddha and commentaries, such as the Uttara Tantra, that have been written in accordance with the teachings. Therefore, by careful study of the Uttara Tantra, prajna will flourish and we will be able to achieve the quality of perfect realization. Hence, this activity accumulates tremendous merit.

What kind of teachings are included in the first category — the words of the Buddha? First, such a teaching must be extremely profound and meaningful. Secondly, the teaching must be in harmony with truth and be, therefore, naturally beneficial. Thirdly, the teaching must pacify the disturbing emotions. Fourthly, the teaching must show the path to peace and happiness. In other words, if a teaching is meaningless, increases disturbing emotions, and leads away from peace and happiness, then it cannot be classified as the words of the Buddha.

Must we rely solely upon the words of the Buddha himself? Not necessarily. We can also place our trust in the commentaries and treatises composed by the learned and accomplished followers of Lord Buddha. But how can we identify a reliable scripture or treatise? If a composition emphasizes a teaching given by the Buddha, himself, as its main theme and clarifies the path to liberation, we can qualify such a treatise as reliable. We should beware of a composition that is written by an author who is merely seeking fame, honor, or wealth.

In short, Lord Maitreya composed the Uttara Tantra which is based on the Buddha's own statements so that countless sentient beings might accumulate an immense store of merit through studying this teaching. Furthermore, studying the Uttara Tantra increases the accumulation of wisdom, or prajna. Once our accumulation of merit and wisdom is increased, we will be able to abandon all that should be abandoned, realize all that should be realized, and uncover our true identity — buddha nature.

Glossary

ABHIDHARMA (chos mngon pa) One of the three sections of the Tripitaka, the Words of the Buddha, the essence of which is *prajna,* discriminating knowledge.

ABHISAMAYA LAMKARA (mngon rtogs rgyan) The *Ornament of Realization* authored by Maitreya and written down by Asanga. It explains the paths and bhumis of the bodhisattva vehicle.

ACHARYA NAGARJUNA (slob dpon klu sgrub) A great Indian master of philosophy, he was named 'Naga Master' because he taught the beings in the naga world. Later, he returned to this world with the extensive version of the *Prajnaparamita* which had been left with them for safekeeping.

ALAYA (kun gzhi) The basis of all of samsara and nirvana. See 'all-ground.'

ALL-GROUND (kun gzhi; alaya) The basis of mind and both pure and impure phenomena. This word has different meanings in different contexts and should, therefore, be understood accordingly. Literally, it means the 'foundation of all things.'

ANUTTARA YOGA (bla na med pa) The unexcelled, highest yoga; the fourth of the four sections of Tantra according to the New Schools.

ARHANT (dgra bcom pa) *Foe destroyer;* someone who has attained the final result of the Hinayana path.

BHUMI (sa) The levels or stages of bodhisattvas; the last three of the *five paths* include ten stages.

BODHGAYA (Skt.) The site situated in Bihar, India where Lord Buddha attained complete enlightenment.

BODHICHITTA (byang sems, byang chub kyi sems) The aspiration to attain enlightenment for the sake of all sentient beings.

BODHISATTVA (byang chub sems dpa') A practitioner of the Mahayana path — especially one who has attained the first bhumi.

BRAHMA (tshangs pa) The chief god in the Realm of Form.

123

BRAHMA LOKA (tshangs pa'i 'jig rten) The samsaric realms of the god, Brahma, within the Realm of Form.

BUDDHA-NATURE (bde gshegs snying po) *Sugata-essence*, the essence of the sugatas; the enlightened nature, or the potential for enlightenment, inherently present in each sentient being.

CHARYA (spyod pa) The second of the *four sections of Tantra.*

COEMERGENT IGNORANCE (lhan cig skyes pa'i ma rig pa) The ignorance which all sentient beings are born with.

DHARMADHATU (chos kyi dbyings) The 'realm of phenomena;' the *suchness* in which emptiness and dependent origination are inseparable. In this context, *Dharma* means 'truth' and *dhatu* means 'space free from center or periphery.' Another explanation is 'the nature of phenomena beyond arising, dwelling, and ceasing.'

DHARMAKAYA (chos sku) The first of the three kayas which is, like space, devoid of all constructs. The nature of all phenomena designated as 'body.' Also, the 'body' of the twenty-one categories of enlightened qualities.

DHARMAKIRTI (chos kyi grags pa) One of the great Buddhist scholars of ancient India.

DHARMATA (chos nyid) The nature of phenomena and mind.

DHYANA (bsam gtan) The fifth of the *Six Paramitas* which means 'steady mindfulness.' Can also refer to the state of concentrated mind with fixation and also the god realms produced through such mental concentration.

DIGNAGA (phyogs glang) Among the *Six Ornaments which Beautify Jambu Continent*, he was the recipient of the transmission of *pramana* — the 'valid cognition' that brings an end to confusion about meaning.

DISCERNING DHARMAS AND DHARMATA (chos dang chos nyid rnam par 'byed pa) One of the *Five Teachings of Maitreya.*

DISCERNING THE MIDDLE AND THE EXTREMES (dbus mtha' rnam par 'byed pa) One of the *Five Teachings of Maitreya.*

DZOGCHEN (rdzogs pa chen po, rdzogs chen) The teachings, beyond the vehicles of causation, which were first taught in the world of human beings by the great vidyadhara, Garab Dorje.

EMPTINESS (stong pa nyid) The fact that phenomena lack any true inherent existence.

FATHER TANTRA (pha rgyud) One of the three aspects of *Anuttara Yoga* which emphasize the development stage.

FIRST TURNING OF THE WHEEL OF DHARMA (chos 'khor dang po) The teachings given by Buddha Shakyamuni which focus on renunciation, karma, and the *Four Noble Truths.*

FIVE AGGREGATES (phung po lnga) The five aspects which comprise the physical and mental constituents of a sentient being: physical form, sensations, conceptions, formations, and consciousnesses.

FIVE PATHS (lam lnga) The paths of *accumulation, joining, seeing, cultivation*, and *no more training.* The five paths cover the entire process from beginning Dharma practice to complete enlightenment.

FIVE SCIENCES (rig gnas lnga) Grammar, logic, craftsmanship, healing, and spirituality.

FOUR SECTIONS OF TANTRA (rgyud sde bzhi) Kriya, Charya, Yoga, and Anuttara Yoga.

FOUR YOGAS OF MAHAMUDRA (phyag chen gyi rnal 'byor bzhi) The four stages in the practice of Mahamudra called *one-pointedness, simplicity, one taste,* and *nonmeditation.*

GAMPOPA (rje btsun sgam po pa) The great forefather of all the Kagyü lineages. See *Life of Milarepa* and *Rain of Wisdom,* both Shambhala Publications.

GARAB DORJE (dga' rab rdo rje; Prahevajra/ Pramoda Vajra) The forefather of the Dzogchen lineage who received the transmission directly from Vajrasattva.

GELUK (dge lugs) The Tibetan school of Buddhism founded by Lord Tsongkhapa as a reformation of the tradition of Atisha Dipamkara. His Holiness the XIV Dalai Lama is the present head of this school.

HINAYANA (theg pa dman pa) The vehicles which, for the sake of gaining individual liberation, focus on the contemplation of the *Four Noble Truths* and the 'twelve links of dependent origination.'

INDRA (brgya byin) The chief god in the Realm of Desire.

INNATE WAKEFULNESS (ye shes) The mind's undeluded and intrinsic capacity of nonconceptual knowing. Usually translated as 'wisdom.'

JAMGÖN KONGTRÜL THE FIRST (byams mgon kong sprul) A great nineteenth century nonsectarian Buddhist master and author of more than one hundred books.

JONANGPA (jo nang pa) Another name for Jetsün Taranatha.

JONANGPA SCHOOL (jo nang pa'i lugs) The school founded by Jetsün Taranatha which asserts that the buddha nature is eternal and unchanging.

KAGYÜ (bka' brgyud) The lineage of teachings brought to Tibet by Marpa the Translator.

KARMA (las) The unerring law of cause and effect whereby all wholesome actions yield wholesome results and unwholesome actions yield unwholesome results.

KARMAPA (kar ma pa) The great Buddhist master and chief figure of the Karma Kagyü school.

KRIYA YOGA (bya ba'i rnal 'byor) The first of the Three Outer Tantras which emphasize cleanliness, pure conduct, and so forth.

KUSULU (Skt.) As opposed to a scholarly person, this is a simple practitioner who merely eats, sleeps, and sits.

LUMINOSITY ('od gsal) Literally, 'freed from the darkness of unknowing and endowed with the ability to cognize,' it is the uncompounded nature present throughout all of samsara and nirvana.

MADHYAMIKA (dbu ma) The Middle (Way). The highest of the four Buddhist schools of philosophy. The Middle Way means 'not holding extreme views, such as eternalism or nihilism.'

MAHAMUDRA (phyag rgya chen po) Literally *The Great Seal*, Mahamudra is the most direct practice for realizing one's buddha nature. A system of teachings comprising the basic view of Vajrayana practice according to the Sarma or New Schools: the Kagyü, Geluk, and Sakya.

MAHAYANA (theg pa chen po) The bodhisattva vehicle which advocates striving for perfect enlightenment for the sake of all sentient beings. For a detailed explanation, see Maitreya's *Ornament of Realization, Abhisamaya Lamkara*.

MAITRIPA (mai tri pa) A great Indian master and one of Marpa the Translator's teachers.

MARA (bdud) Demon or demonic influence that creates obstacles for practice and the attainment of enlightenment.

MARPA THE TRANSLATOR (mar pa lo tsa ba) The great forefather of the Kagyü lineage. See *Life of Marpa the Translator,* Shambhala Publications.

MILAREPA (mi la ras pa) A great yogin and major Kagyü lineage-holder. A Tibetan Buddhist master and the chief disciple of Marpa the Translator. See *Life of Milarepa* translated by L. Lhalungpa, Shambhala Publications.

MIND-ONLY SCHOOL (sems tsam pa, Chitta-matra) A Mahayana school of India.

MOTHER TANTRA (ma rgyud) One of the three aspects of Anuttara Yoga which emphasizes the completion stage.

NAGARJUNA (klu grub) An Indian master of philosophy. See Acharya Nagarjuna.

NALANDA (Skt.) The great monastic center for Buddhist studies in ancient India.

NAROPA (na ro pa) The great mahasiddha of India, chief disciple of Tilopa, and guru of Marpa in the Kagyü Lineage. See *Rain of Wisdom,* Shambhala Publications.

NEW AND OLD SCHOOLS (gsar rnying) The New Schools are Kagyü, Sakya, and Geluk. The Old School refers to Nyingma.

NINE YANAS (theg pa dgu) The nine gradual vehicles: the general vehicles for shravakas, pratyekabuddhas, and bodhisattvas, the outer tantric vehicles of Kriya, Charya, and Yoga, and the inner tantric vehicles of Maha, Anu, and Ati.

NIRMANAKAYA (sprul sku) *Emanation body.* The third of the three kayas. The aspect of enlightenment that tames beings and can be perceived by ordinary beings.

NONDUAL TANTRA (gnyis med rgyud) The third of the three aspects of *Anuttara Yoga* which emphasizes the unity of the stages of development and completion.

NYINGMA SCHOOL (rnying ma) The Buddhist school which has preserved the teachings brought to Tibet and translated chiefly during the reign of King Trisong Deutsen and in the following period up to Rinchen Sangpo.

POINTING-OUT INSTRUCTION (ngo sprod kyi gdams pa) The direct introduction to the nature of mind.

PRAJNA (shes rab) Knowledge or intelligence. In particular, the 'knowledge of realizing egolessness.'

PRATYEKABUDDHA (rang sangs rgyas) *Solitary Enlightened One.* A person who has reached perfection in the second Hinayana vehicle chiefly through contemplation on the twelve links of dependent origination in reverse order.

RIGPA (Tib. rig pa) The state of awareness devoid of ignorance and dualistic fixation.

RUPAKAYA (gzugs kyi sku) *Form body.* A collective term for both *sambhoga-kaya* and *nirmanakaya.*

SAKYAPA (sa skya pa) A follower of the Sakya lineage of Tibetan Buddhism.

SAMADHI (ting nge 'dzin) 'Adhering to the continuity or evenness.' Usually translated as concentration or meditative absorption.

SAMANTABHADRA (kun tu bzang po) The *Ever-excellent One.* The primordial dharmakaya buddha.

SAMBHOGAKAYA (longs spyod rdzogs pa'i sku) The 'body of perfect enjoy-ment.' Of the five kayas of fruition, it is the semi-manifest form of the buddhas endowed with the *five perfections*: perfect teacher, retinue, place, teaching, and time which is perceptible only to bodhisattvas on the ten bhumis.

SAMSARA ('khor ba) 'Cyclic existence,' 'vicious circle,' or 'round' of births and deaths. The state of ordinary sentient beings fettered by ignorance and dualistic perception, karma and disturbing emotions.

SECOND TURNING OF THE WHEEL OF DHARMA (chos 'khor gnyis pa) The teachings which emphasize *emptiness* — that all phenomena are devoid of a self-entity and lack any true existence.

SENTIENT BEINGS (sems can) Any living being in one of the six realms who has not attained liberation.

SHAMATHA (zhi gnas) 'Calm abiding' or 'remaining in quiescence' after thought activity has subsided; the meditative practice of calming the mind in order to rest free from the disturbance of thought.

SHRAVAKA (nyan thos) 'Hearer' or 'listener.' The practitioners of the First Turning of the Wheel of the Dharma who chiefly contemplate the Four Noble Truths.

SIX PARAMITAS (phar phyin drug) The six transcendent actions of generosity, discipline, patience, diligence, concentration, and discriminating knowl-edge.

SUCHNESS (de bzhin nyid) Synonym for *emptiness* or the 'nature of things,' *dharmata.* It can also be used to describe the unity of dependent origina-tion and emptiness.

SUGATA-ESSENCE (bde bar gshegs pa'i snying po) *Sugata essence* is the most common Sanskrit term for what in the West is known as 'buddha nature.'

SUTRA (mdo) Discourse or teaching given by Buddha Shakyamuni. Can also refer to all the causal teachings that take the causes for buddhahood as path.

SUTRA LAMKARA (mdo sde rgyan) *The Ornament of the Sutras,* one of the *Five Teachings of Maitreya.*

TANTRA (rgyud) The Vajrayana teachings given by Buddha Shakyamuni in his sambhogakaya form. Literally, 'continuity,' tantra means the buddha nature, the 'tantra of the expressed meaning.' Generally a tantric scripture, the 'tantra of the expressing words.' Can also refer to all the resultant teachings that take the result as the path as a whole.

TARANATHA: See 'Jonangpa.'

TATHAGATA-ESSENCE (de bzhin gshegs pa'i snying po) Same as the 'buddha nature' and *sugata-essence.*

THIRD TURNING OF THE WHEEL OF DHARMA (chos 'khor gsum pa) The teachings by the Buddha which emphasize the buddha nature, the unity of luminosity and emptiness devoid of constructs, and which include the sutras on the definitive meaning.

THREE JEWELS (dkon mchog gsum) The Precious Buddha, the Precious Dharma, and the Precious Sangha.

TILOPA: An Indian mahasiddha, the guru of Naropa, and forefather of the Kagyü lineage.

TULKU (sprul sku) Literally, 'apparitional body.' Can refer to an incarnated bodhisattva who works for the welfare of sentient beings, or to the nirma-nakaya manifested by a buddha.

TUSHITA HEAVEN (dga' ldan) The heavenly realm in which Lord Maitreya resides while waiting to appear in this world as the next Buddha.

TWELVE DEEDS (mdzad pa bcu gnyis) For a detailed story of the Buddha's twelve deeds, see the *Lalitavistara Sutra,* Dharma Publishing 1983.

VAJRALIKE SAMADHI (rdo rje lta bu'i ting nge 'dzin) The final stage of the tenth bhumi which results in buddhahood.

VAJRADHARA (rdo rje 'chang) *Vajra-holder.* The dharmakaya buddha of the Sarma Schools. Can also refer to one's personal teacher of Vajrayana.

VAJRAYANA (rdo rje theg pa) The 'vajra vehicle.' The practices of taking the result as the path.

VICTORIOUS ONES (rgyal ba, jina) Synonym for the buddhas.

VINAYA ('dul ba) 'Discipline.' One of the three sections of the Tripitaka.

VIPASHYANA (lhag mthong) 'Clear' or 'wider seeing.' One of the two main aspects of meditation practice, the other being *shamatha.*

YIDAM (yi dam) A personal deity and, among the Three Roots, the root of accomplishment.

YOGA (rnal 'byor) The third of the Three Outer Tantras: *Kriya,* Charya, and *Yoga.*